TIME

The New Middle East

After the Arab Spring, a different world unfolds.

A protester in Cairo throws a
tear gas canister—which had
earlier been lobbed by riot police
—in the days leading up to Egypt's
first free election in decades.

TIME

MANAGING EDITOR Richard Stengel
DESIGN DIRECTOR D.W. Pine
DIRECTOR OF PHOTOGRAPHY Kira Pollack

The New Middle East
After the Arab Spring, a different world unfolds.

EDITOR Bobby Ghosh
DESIGNER Sharon Okamoto
PHOTO EDITOR Dot McMahon
HEAD REPORTER Cleo Brock-Abraham
EDITORIAL PRODUCTION Lionel Vargas
GRAPHICS EDITOR Lon Tweeten

TIME HOME ENTERTAINMENT

PUBLISHER Richard Fraiman
VICE PRESIDENT, BUSINESS DEVELOPMENT AND STRATEGY Steven Sandonato
EXECUTIVE DIRECTOR, MARKETING SERVICES Carol Pittard
EXECUTIVE DIRECTOR, RETAIL AND SPECIAL SALES Tom Mifsud
EXECUTIVE DIRECTOR, NEW PRODUCT DEVELOPMENT Peter Harper
DIRECTOR, BOOKAZINE DEVELOPMENT AND MARKETING Laura Adam
PUBLISHING DIRECTOR Joy Butts
FINANCE DIRECTOR Glenn Buonocore
ASSISTANT GENERAL COUNSEL Helen Wan
ASSISTANT DIRECTOR, SPECIAL SALES Ilene Schreider
BOOK PRODUCTION MANAGER Suzanne Janso
DESIGN AND PREPRESS MANAGER Anne-Michelle Gallero
BRAND MANAGER Michela Wilde

EDITORIAL DIRECTOR Stephen Koepp

SPECIAL THANKS TO:
Christine Austin, Jeremy Biloon, Jim Childs, Susan Chodakiewicz, Rose Cirrincione,
Jacqueline Fitzgerald, Carrie Hertan, Hillary Hirsch, Christine Font,
Jenna Goldberg, Lauren Hall Clark, Amy Mangus, Robert Marasco,
Kimberly Marshall, Amy Migliaccio, Nina Mistry, Tara Rice, Dave Rozzelle,
Adriana Tierno, Alex Voznesenskiy, Vanessa Wu, TIME Imaging

ISBN 13: 978-1-61893-023-1
ISBN 10: 1-61893-023-0
Library of Congress Control Number: 2012931011

We welcome your comments and suggestions about TIME Books. Please write to us at:
TIME Books, Attention: Book Editors, P.O. Box 11016, Des Moines, IA 50336-1016

If you would like to order any of our hardcover Collector's Edition books, please call us at
1-800-327-6388, Monday through Friday, 7 a.m. to 8 p.m., or Saturday, 7 a.m. to 6 p.m., Central Time.

Contents

Anti-Gaddafi rebels raise their flag in Ras Lanus in March 2011.

Cairene women show off ink-stained fingers after voting in free elections.

Revolution 2.0

BY REZA ASLAN

M Y FAMILY LEFT IRAN JUST A FEW MONTHS AFTER A POPULAR uprising, mostly made up of young democracy activists, managed to topple the country's corrupt, Western-backed dictator, Muhammad Reza Pahlavi. Having been on the streets of Tehran in those heady days in the late 1970s, I witnessed for myself the camaraderie and sense of common purpose that drove a diverse coalition of Iranians to risk their lives for the possibility of freedom and democracy. Yes, there were religious forces among the crowd. But contrary to popular perception, they did not conduct the choir of voices raised against the Shah; they were merely part of the grand chorus made up of Marxists and socialists, communists and democrats, secularists and theocrats,

Muslims, Christians, Jews, men, women, and children—all of them united by a single overriding ambition: to cast off the yoke of authoritarianism and rebuild the country anew. Yet when we arrived in the U.S., I was immediately confronted with an image of the Iranian revolution in the American media that was completely at odds with what I had experienced on the ground in Tehran. I remember watching an aged American news anchor perched behind his desk, reading a Teleprompter with all the authority of a pope, as images of angry, bearded mullahs flashed across the screen. I remember, too, the parade of pundits and politicians who flooded the airwaves to warn Americans about the fanatics taking over my country. In their telling, it was not a revolution, it was a coup. It was not democracy, it was radical Islam.

And when a group of zealous Iranian students stormed the U.S. embassy and took Americans hostage, the narrative about the revolution was set in stone. By the time Iraq's Saddam Hussein (encouraged by the U.S.) launched a surprise attack on Iran, that narrative had become a self-fulfilling prophecy. The democratic transitional government was ousted, and the vibrant debate about the function and nature of post-revolutionary Iran came to an end as power was centralized in the hands of the only man who could wield it in the midst of the chaos: the Ayatollah Khomeini.

I've been thinking a lot about that experience as I've watched the images of the popular uprisings in Tunisia, Egypt, Libya, Syria, Bahrain, Oman, and beyond. During the early days of the Arab Spring, the rhetoric from many pundits and politicians sounded eerily familiar. Indeed, many in the news media explicitly cited the example of Iran in warning of the threat posed by the Arab revolutions to American values and interests.

But things are different now. Much has been written about the role that social media have played in allowing people in the Middle East to communicate with one another and with the outside world. Some have even referred to the Arab Spring as the Facebook or Twitter revolution. Less discussed is the way the Internet and social media have shattered the American media's monopoly over information and therefore over people's impressions and opinions about world events. For the first time Americans were able to hear directly from people on the streets in Tunis, Cairo, Benghazi, and Homs without the filter of a nightly newscast. They were able to experience for themselves, in real time, the struggle of a young, desperate, and downtrodden population willing to risk everything to achieve the basic rights and freedoms most Americans take for granted.

All of this is to remind us that the tools that made the Arab revolutions possible are global; their effects have been felt everywhere—from Moscow to Zuccotti Park. Simply put, we are not witnessing an Arab revolution, but a global revolution, one whose lasting impact on the world is difficult to imagine. Think of it this way: What if those tens of thousands of Chinese youth who gathered in Tiananmen Square two decades ago to demand freedom and democracy had had Twitter? What would China look like today? What would the world look like?

The events of the Arab Spring have forever transformed the Middle East. And while we may not know exactly what shape the region will take in the years to come, we recognize that the revolutions that began in 2011 are very much still underway. The economy is floundering in Tunisia. Egypt still suffers under military rule. Libya has no real government to speak of. And Syrians have been dying in the streets. It remains to be seen whether populations that have lived so long under the boot of dictatorship can put aside their differences and build a truly free and democratic society. But this much is certain: The Arab Spring has taught us all that in a world in which a single individual or group can no longer control the free flow of information, no authority—be it an Arab dictator, a Russian tycoon, or an American corporation—is immune to the power of a people united in the cause of justice. *–Reza Aslan is the founder of AslanMedia.com and author of* No god but God, Beyond Fundamentalism, *and* Tablet & Pen.

A Region Rises

The Arab Spring didn't just bring down a few dictators: Across the Middle East, it changed the way ruler and ruled saw each other.

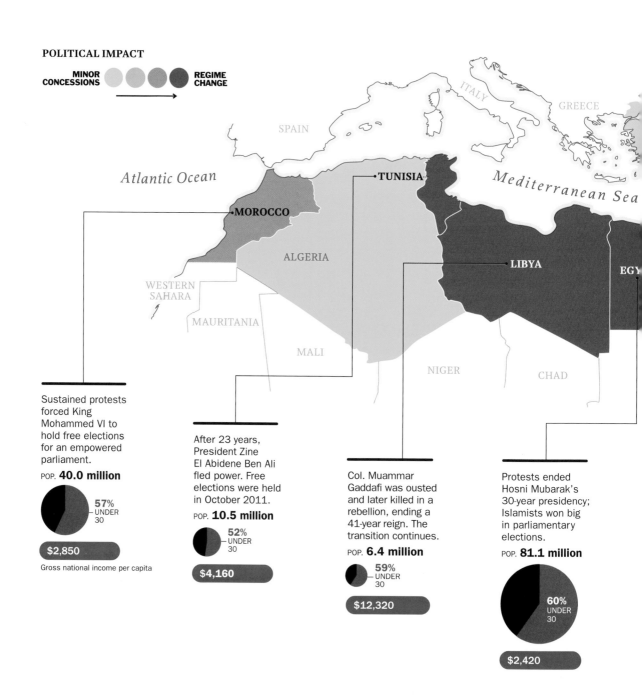

POLITICAL IMPACT

MINOR CONCESSIONS → REGIME CHANGE

Sustained protests forced King Mohammed VI to hold free elections for an empowered parliament.

POP. **40.0 million**

57% UNDER 30

$2,850

Gross national income per capita

After 23 years, President Zine El Abidene Ben Ali fled power. Free elections were held in October 2011.

POP. **10.5 million**

52% UNDER 30

$4,160

Col. Muammar Gaddafi was ousted and later killed in a rebellion, ending a 41-year reign. The transition continues.

POP. **6.4 million**

59% UNDER 30

$12,320

Protests ended Hosni Mubarak's 30-year presidency; Islamists won big in parliamentary elections.

POP. **81.1 million**

60% UNDER 30

$2,420

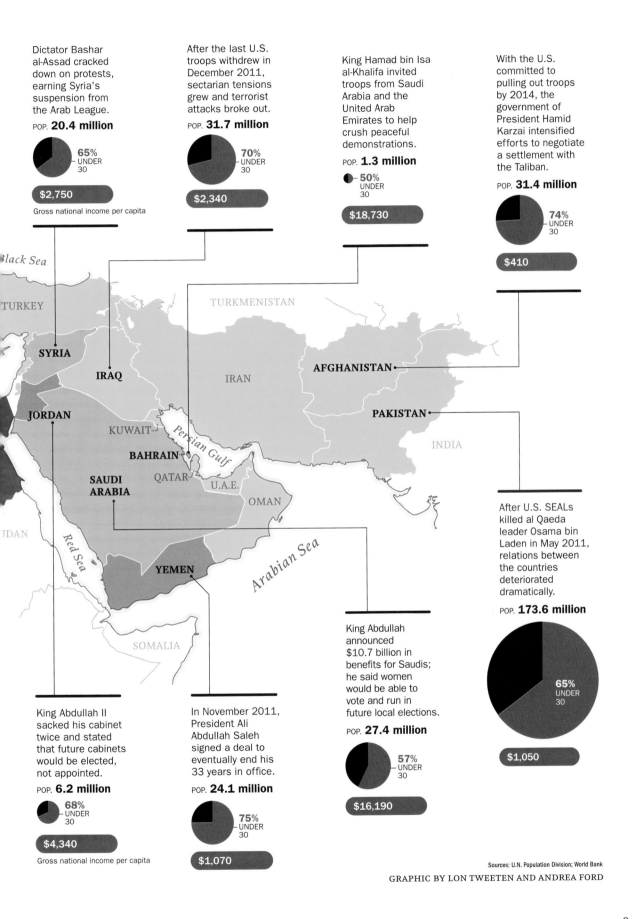

Dictator Bashar al-Assad cracked down on protests, earning Syria's suspension from the Arab League.

POP. **20.4 million**

65% UNDER 30

$2,750

Gross national income per capita

After the last U.S. troops withdrew in December 2011, sectarian tensions grew and terrorist attacks broke out.

POP. **31.7 million**

70% UNDER 30

$2,340

King Hamad bin Isa al-Khalifa invited troops from Saudi Arabia and the United Arab Emirates to help crush peaceful demonstrations.

POP. **1.3 million**

50% UNDER 30

$18,730

With the U.S. committed to pulling out troops by 2014, the government of President Hamid Karzai intensified efforts to negotiate a settlement with the Taliban.

POP. **31.4 million**

74% UNDER 30

$410

Black Sea

TURKEY

TURKMENISTAN

SYRIA

IRAQ

IRAN

AFGHANISTAN

PAKISTAN

JORDAN

KUWAIT

Persian Gulf

INDIA

BAHRAIN

SAUDI ARABIA

QATAR

U.A.E.

OMAN

JDAN

Red Sea

Arabian Sea

YEMEN

SOMALIA

After U.S. SEALs killed al Qaeda leader Osama bin Laden in May 2011, relations between the countries deteriorated dramatically.

POP. **173.6 million**

65% UNDER 30

$1,050

King Abdullah announced $10.7 billion in benefits for Saudis; he said women would be able to vote and run in future local elections.

POP. **27.4 million**

57% UNDER 30

$16,190

King Abdullah II sacked his cabinet twice and stated that future cabinets would be elected, not appointed.

POP. **6.2 million**

68% UNDER 30

$4,340

Gross national income per capita

In November 2011, President Ali Abdullah Saleh signed a deal to eventually end his 33 years in office.

POP. **24.1 million**

75% UNDER 30

$1,070

Sources: U.N. Population Division; World Bank

GRAPHIC BY LON TWEETEN AND ANDREA FORD

Generation A

The Arab world's young people, emboldened by their numbers and inflamed by economic frustration, overthrew the autocrats and the old social order. Inside the youthquake that launched a new era in the Middle East.

Armed with cellphones, young Tunisians gathered in January 2011 to demand that their dictator step down.

Youth

The Young
and the Restless

*How the "youth bulge," joblessness, and the
decadent lifestyles of dictators finally set the stage
for a revolution that spanned a region.*

BY BOBBY GHOSH

I 'LL ADMIT IT: I DIDN'T THINK THE KIDS HAD REVOLUTION IN THEM. LIKE MOST
Middle East "experts," I was dismissive of young Arabs. In more than a decade of traveling across the region, I had rarely encountered young men or women who were trying to
change the status quo, unless you counted the deluded jihadists who thought they could
simply blow it up. For the most part, Arab youth seemed apathetic and supine. They took
little interest in politics and shrugged off the corruption and misrule of their rulers. They
had plenty of cause to rebel but seemed unwilling or unable to do it.

Why? Some political scientists argued that despotic Arab regimes had cowed the youth into
submission. Any revolutionary zeal that might have existed in young minds was rubbed out by
fear of imprisonment and torture by the pervasive state security apparatus. Another theory suggested that young Arabs were infected by the disillusionment of their parents, who had tried their
hand at revolution in the 1950s and '60s, only to see their revolutionary leaders themselves turn
into autocrats—like Libya's Muammar Gaddafi, Egypt's Gamal
Abdel Nasser, and the Ba'ath Party of Iraq and Syria.

I remember a conversation about youthful apathy with
an Iraqi tribal sheikh just outside the southern city of Basra. It
was the spring of 2003, and the U.S.-led invasion was just days
away. When my government-appointed minder was distracted
for a few minutes, the sheikh said he was looking forward to

Bobby Ghosh, TIME's *deputy international editor, has reported extensively from
the Middle East and lived in Baghdad from 2003 to 2007.*

*Rebels for a cause: (clockwise from
bottom right) Tunisian El General
wrote the revolution's rap anthem;
Egyptian-American journalist Mona
Eltahawy endured assault by police;
Egyptian Um Treka protested from
behind the veil; activists Abdulhamid
Sulaiman, Rami Jarrah, and
Mohamed Abazid helped keep the
world's attention on their native Syria.*

Mannoubia Bouazizi's son Mohamed sparked a revolution when he set himself afire to protest police corruption and official apathy in his Tunisian hometown of Sidi Bouzid.

14

war—only a foreign army, he reasoned, could topple Saddam Hussein. Why can't Iraqis rise up against the tyrant? I asked. The sheikh, who had 11 children, several of them young adults, shook his head ruefully. "Our young people are too patient," he said. "They wait and wait and wait for change. But patience is not a good weapon to use against dictators."

That patience ran out at the start of 2011, when Arab youth finally stood up to their dictators. By year's end, they had toppled three tyrants: Tunisia's Zine El Abidine Ben Ali, Egypt's Hosni Mubarak, and Libya's Gaddafi. A fourth, Yemen's Ali Abdullah Saleh, had agreed to quit. And Syria's Bashar al-Assad looked shakier than at any other time in the four decades that he and his father before him had ruled the country.

Even in countries where the rulers remained unchanged, the Arab Spring had a profound impact. In Morocco street protests persuaded the king to allow free elections for the first time. Jordan's monarch, rattled by similar demonstrations, twice dismissed his entire cabinet as a concession to angry citizens. Even the all-powerful Saudi Arabian royal family felt compelled to preempt any reform movement by handing out tens of billions of dollars of largesse.

The long-standing compact between ruler and ruled had changed, very likely forever. And it was those supposedly apathetic young men and women who had made it possible. Everywhere the revolution was led by the youth. Mohamed Bouazizi, 26, a Tunisian vegetable vendor, lit the spark by setting himself on fire as a protest against corruption and oppression. The flame was carried forward by activists like Tunisia's Lina ben Mhenni, 27, and Egypt's Ahmed Maher, 31, who used modern social media tools like Facebook and Twitter to organize street protests. Others, like Yemen's Tawakkul Karman, 33, displayed steely nerves in the face of government oppression and carried on protesting for months on end. (Karman ended the year as the first Arab woman to receive the Nobel Peace Prize.)

What happened? How did a generation that was supposedly uninterested in politics become the vanguard of the greatest political upheaval since the collapse of the Soviet Union?

There seem to be as many explanations as there are revolutionaries—and there are a lot of those. Arab populations have exploded in the decades since the last wave of revolutions. There are now around 350 million people in 22 Arab nations, or nearly three times the population in 1970. (Over that same period, the population of the U.S. grew 52%, aided by immigration.)

That growth spurt means a disproportionate number of Arabs are young. Social scientists use the term "youth bulge" to describe an unusually large proportion of a nation's population being ages 15 to 29. Some suggest the demographic anomaly set the stage for social upheaval. In North Africa and the Middle East, an astonishing 60% of the population is under 30, or roughly twice the proportion in North America.

Countries with a youth bulge often struggle to find enough jobs for their young people. Crippled by corruption and ineptitude, most Middle Eastern economies—especially those not blessed with giant oil and gas deposits—barely bothered to make an effort at job creation. In Egypt the rewards of economic reform and growth were restricted to cronies of Mubarak and his son Gamal. In Libya the windfall profits from the rise in oil prices were swallowed almost whole by Gaddafi's clan. As a result, youth unemployment across the region ranged from 25% to 40%.

Joblessness on such a large scale leaves a profound mark on society. Young people are obliged to live with their parents much longer than their peers in other countries. Marriage becomes an unobtainable luxury. Radical and violent ideologies that promise an escape from despair grow popular.

But by the end of the last decade, jihad had become thoroughly discredited as a revolutionary ideology. Islamist groups like Egypt's Muslim Brotherhood had long since renounced violence, Osama bin Laden was hiding in Pakistan, and suicide bombings had failed to deliver political change. On the other hand, peaceful protest had freed Lebanon from Syrian control, and democracy had provided Iraqis a representative (albeit imperfect) government. Turkey and Indonesia were giving the lie to the old notion that Islam and democracy are mutually exclusive.

Two decades ago Arab autocrats would have been able to keep much of this information from their people, mainly by exercising total control of the local media and barring access to foreign news outlets. But starting in the late 1990s, many Arab states began to allow their citizens access to satellite TV. In retrospect, it was a bad call by dictators; it allowed news channels like Al Jazeera and Al Arabiya, as well as the Arabic-language service of the BBC, to beam revolutionary ideas into the minds of viewers.

Another fateful decision by the likes of Ben Ali and Gaddafi was opening up their markets to Internet and cellphone services. That meant that state censors (many of whom were stuck in the fixed-line-telephone era) could never be sure what people were saying to one another. It's no coincidence that the Syrian regime, with the most sophisticated censorship apparatus of the states in which revolution broke out, has proved most immune.

Other ingredients for revolution began to come together in 2010. The global economic crisis hurt businesses, leading to even more joblessness. A global spike in food prices hit the Middle East especially hard. Families already impoverished by unemployment saw their food bills soar. Frustration escalated. There were several small riots in Egypt over the price of bread.

Already furious with the incompetence and callousness of their rulers, young Arabs suddenly got a glimpse into what was really going on in the presidential palaces. WikiLeaks released a trove of U.S. State Department documents, including reports by ambassadors in the Middle East that described the venality of the first families as well as their lavish lifestyles. Tunisians had long known that the family of President Ben Ali was helping itself to plum state contracts and that First Lady Leila Trabelsi's relatives had grown rich in a suspiciously short time. Now a leaked cable from the American envoy revealed, in excruciating detail, land grabs by Trabelsi, drug dealing by one of Ben Ali's brothers, and the brazen theft of a luxury yacht by two of the president's nephews. One son-in-law threw parties for which ice cream was flown in from Saint-Tropez. The disclosures filled young Tunisians, many of whom were struggling to make ends meet, with revulsion. Libyans, Egyptians, and Yemenis were reading equally unsavory cables, also released by WikiLeaks, about their own rulers.

The stage was set for revolution.

When it began, the revolution's greatest strengths were the passion and tech savvy of its youthful leaders. The "Facebook revolutionaries," as they came to be known, were able to circumvent state censors and snoops by planning demonstrations and sharing information over the Internet. Bloggers posted pictures and video of security crackdowns, and shared advice on how best to avoid police beatings and on remedies for tear gas.

The use of the Internet also allowed the revolution to easily cross borders: Egyptian blogger-activists were able to communicate with their Tunisian counterparts and get tips on how to organize protests. In turn, the Egyptians were able to share with Libyans, Syrians, and Yemenis. When Ben Ali fell, celebrations spread across North Africa and the Middle East. The apathetic generation had scored one victory, and others were on the way. The status quo was no more.

Where do young Arabs go from here? In much of the region, the revolution is still incomplete—some old dictators cling to power.

Where regimes have already been toppled, young people are struggling to find a new role for themselves. In the wake of the Arab Spring, the political landscape is still dominated by the older generation and by Islamist parties. The revolutionaries have proved naive politicians, unable

The artifacts of the revolution included tear-gas canisters and smartphones. Some came off the worse for wear.

to translate their street cred into votes. United in Tahrir Square, they split into small parties and became thoroughly disorganized: Facebook and Twitter are not much use in appealing to an electorate in which the majority don't own computers. In Egypt the Brotherhood has won a plurality in parliament, and the main contenders for the presidency are all in their 60s. The leadership of Ennahda, the Islamist party that won elections in Tunisia, is substantially older than the blogger-activists who rose against Ben Ali.

The challenge for the revolutionaries is to respect the results of the democratic processes revolution made possible. For some, the Islamist victory is hard to swallow, and the temptation is to somehow undermine it. In Cairo, after the first round of voting in the three-stage general election, many young activists told me that too many voters were uneducated and illiterate, so the results would not accurately reflect the people's choice. (This is exactly the sort of thing Mubarak's cronies used to say when the Muslim Brotherhood won seats in the old parliament, despite the regime's best efforts to fix the vote.) In Cairo there was a great deal of talk about a "return to Tahrir Square" to keep any Islamist government on the defensive. Sour grapes don't behoove revolutionaries.

Other activists, more sanguine about the election results, say their work is far from done. Egypt's Maher, for instance, believes young revolutionaries must keep up the pressure on the military to get out of politics and stay out. He and his colleagues are also involved in voter-education programs designed to teach Egyptians about the complexities of democracy. They see themselves as a cross between monitors and conscience-keepers. Indeed, somebody has to make sure the democratic governments quickly get down to the business of cleaning up corruption and creating jobs. It's an important function, one that newborn democracies desperately need. But it calls for very different skills from those that make for a successful revolution. More than anything else, it requires the quality that the Iraqi sheikh cited to me back in 2003: patience. It may be no good against dictators, but it's pretty useful after they're gone.

Tunisia

Wireless Heralds

After an oppressed fruit vendor lit the spark
of revolution, young activists showed the Arab world
how to thwart the censors and mobilize the citizens.

BY BOBBY GHOSH

SIDI BOUZID IS A SLEEPY TOWN OF 40,000 IN CENTRAL TUNISIA, WITH NO distinguishing topography or architecture. It has none of the makings of a cradle of revolution. There are no signs of extreme poverty or of immense wealth. There's no great prison where prisoners may riot against sadistic guards, no great university campus where students may organize for the right to speak freely. But sometimes revolutions can be made on nondescript street corners, and from the simplest ingredients, like a policewoman possessed of casual cruelty and a poor vegetable seller at the end of his rope. On the morning of Dec. 17, 2010, she confiscated his cart, an occupational hazard for street vendors. When he protested, she slapped him. For Mohamed Bouazizi, 26, long cowed by the law, it was one insult too far. Seeking redress, he went to the nearby office of the provincial authority, but nobody there would listen to him. Then he snapped.

Bouazizi found a spot across the street from the office, doused himself with gasoline, and lit a match. It would prove to be the spark of a revolution that fanned across the Arab world and in less than a year toppled three of its most durable dictators.

The vegetable vendor didn't own a smartphone and was too poor to while away the hours in Internet cafés. But those who did were galvanized by his self-immolation. Young Tunisians identified with Bouazizi's desperation: They, too, felt rage and helplessness. The corrupt, inept regime of President Zine El Abidine Ben Ali, Tunisia's ruler for 23 years, had mismanaged the economy to the point where young people had few jobs and fewer prospects. Ben Ali's own family, however, had helped itself to government contracts with multinational companies. Something had to give.

Bouazizi's immolation (and death on Jan. 4, 2011) led to street protests in Sidi Bouzid, but they barely got a mention in the censored Tunisian media. They did, however, catch the attention of a scattered group of young Tunisian activists. People like Lina ben Mhenni, whose Tunisian Girl blog circumvented Ben Ali's old-media censors, told Bouazizi's story on Facebook and Twitter. When

Young Tunisians, like these at an Internet café, were able to use social media tools to organize their revolution.

the protests in Sidi Bouzid were crushed by police, cellphone videos quickly appeared on YouTube.

As more Tunisians logged on to follow the news, activists like Slim Amamou and Bassem Bougerra began to use social media networks not only to spread the word but also to organize: Protests were planned, locations and dates were posted. "At first we didn't know if people would come," Amamou told TIME. "But they came—first hundreds, then thousands, then hundreds of thousands." Text messages on cellphones got the word to those who didn't have Internet access.

Tunisia's dictator responded with pre-web predictability: He cracked down on protests and tried to black out the news. Both failed. Cellphones easily defeated the censors. After initially standing with the dictator, the Tunisian military refused orders to shoot demonstrators. Within 10 days of Bouazizi's death, Ben Ali had fled to Saudi Arabia and resigned as president. Social media networks swiftly carried the revolution across North Africa and the Arab world. Tunisian activists found themselves giving advice to Egyptians, Yemenis, and Syrians. "We became consultants, sharing our experience and expertise," said Bougerra, still marveling at the notion several months after Ben Ali's ouster. "People were asking me, 'How do we clean our eyes after a tear-gas attack?'"

Egyptian bloggers had their own martyr, their equivalent of Mohamed Bouazizi. His name was Khaled Said, and he had been beaten to death by the police in June 2010. Images of his body, bearing clear signs of brutality, had been widely distributed online. But it wasn't until the Tunisian revolution that young Egyptians fully grasped the power of social media. In Cairo, Ahmed Maher, one of the founders of the April 6 movement, remembers reaching out to Tunisian bloggers. "They had accomplished something amazing. They had shown us that young, powerless people could be powerful with these simple tools," he said. "Facebook used to be a place where we went to get away from our frustrations. Now it became the place we could find the solution to our frustrations."

Mohamed Bouazizi would have approved.

In late 2011, political campaigns bloomed in neighborhoods like Cairo's Talaat Harb, named for a revered Egyptian economist.

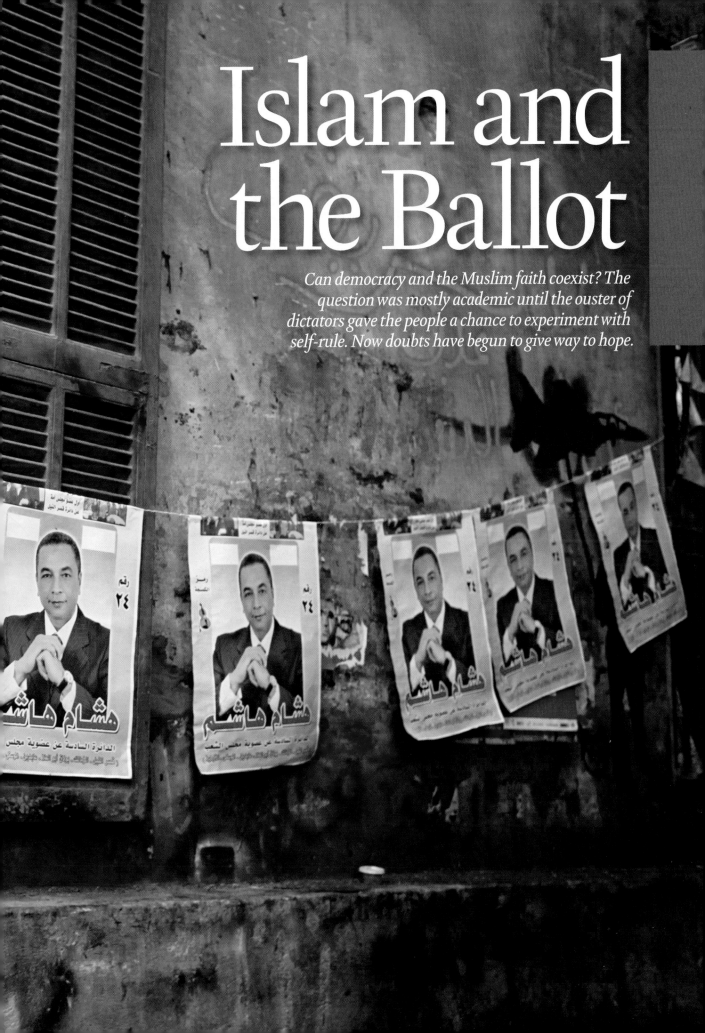

Islam and the Ballot

Can democracy and the Muslim faith coexist? The question was mostly academic until the ouster of dictators gave the people a chance to experiment with self-rule. Now doubts have begun to give way to hope.

In Cairo's Tahrir Square, an antigovernment demonstrator gets a lift from the euphoric throng.

Egypt

The Soaring Crescent

*Political freedoms won in a largely secular
revolution have brought Islamist parties to power
in the Arab world's most important country. But
do they have the answers to its great problems?*

BY ABIGAIL HAUSLOHNER

BEFORE "TAHRIR SQUARE" BECAME A HOUSEHOLD name around the world, Egypt was often described as the most reliably stagnant country in the modern Middle East. Octogenarian President Hosni Mubarak had ruled the Arab world's largest nation for nearly three decades, and had kept an iron grip on power through a pervasive security apparatus. Most of the country's 85 million people abstained from the sham democracy that Mubarak maintained for the sake of his Western partners and critics, and his corruption-tainted economy grew at a rate that was just pleasing enough to foreign investors, while doing little to improve the lot of a seemingly placid populace, 40% of whom subsisted on less than $2 a day.

That superficial stability was shattered in the first two months of 2011. Egyptians took to the streets for 18 days, and took the world by surprise in what became the first truly popular uprising in the country's history. Their success at toppling the Mubarak regime sent shock waves through the region and helped accelerate a global protest movement that had begun in Tunisia and would spread in various guises from Moscow's Red Square to New York's Zuccotti Park.

Why was Egypt critical to the Arab Spring? Because the land of the Nile, home to one of the world's oldest civilizations, has always exercised tremendous influence on how the rest of the Middle East thinks, thanks to its movies and television shows, which are watched in all Arabic-speaking countries. Egypt is also vital to U.S. foreign policy: It is one of only two Arab countries to formally make peace with Israel (the other is Jordan), and is the second-largest recipient of American military aid after Israel. Its airspace and Suez Canal are crucial to American strategic interests, especially during the Iraq war, and given rising tensions with Iran, again now.

The unlikely downfall of Tunisian President Zine El Abidine Ben Ali in January 2011 was a watershed moment for Egyptians. Inspired, the country's weak and fractured opposition movement planned its own "Day of Rage" protests for Jan. 25. But the frustrations of the silent majority had already reached a boiling point. The cost of living had skyrocketed in recent years, even as food shortages had worsened and as Mubarak's cronies appeared to be growing richer. The 2010 beating death of a young man named Khaled Said at the hands of plainclothes police had, thanks to social media activists, galvanized the consciousness of Egypt's long-apathetic youth. So on Jan. 25, hundreds of thousands massed in the streets, chanting slogans against the regime. Mubarak struck back with violence, but he miscalculated the level of dissent. Within days, Egyptians had forced the nationwide retreat of the police force, set the ruling party headquarters on fire, and taken control of Tahrir Square in downtown Cairo. After three weeks of protests, crackdowns, and yet more protests, Mubarak stepped down and ceded control of the country to a shadowy group of his top generals known as the Supreme Council of the Armed Forces (SCAF). Egyptians were elated and stunned by their own success.

In the aftermath of revolution, the euphoria quickly evolved into apprehension about Egypt's prospects for a free, secure, and democratic future. Civil unrest, border insecurity, protests, and labor strikes continued to rock the country. Corruption was still rampant in virtually every sector. Public infrastructure, including schools and hospitals, operated in squalid conditions. And the economy, which depends heavily on tourism, plummeted into crisis mode, with an estimated deficit of $22 billion for 2012, or 8.6% of gross domestic product. The rising prices, fuel shortages, and unrelenting poverty represented "a ticking time bomb," said Hisham Kassem, a leading journalist.

The now iconic Tahrir Square remained a focal point for protest. With Mubarak gone, demonstrators directed their wrath at the military leadership, which seemed determined to hold on to power and periodically came down hard on the protesters. Hundreds have been killed, and thousands of others have been tried before military courts.

The group that made the best of Mubarak's ouster were Egypt's Islamists, who metamorphosed from a repressed and battered opposition movement into the country's most powerful political players. The Muslim Brotherhood, banned under the previous regime, took advantage of the new freedoms to swiftly spread its influence. Founded in 1928 by the Islamic scholar Hassan al-Banna, the Brotherhood spent decades challenging Egypt's authoritarian system and British colonial overseers, driven by a quest for a moral Islamic society. The group's Islamist ideology has inspired the establishment of Brotherhood branches across the Muslim world, as well as violent offshoots like Hamas and al Qaeda.

Initially striving to change society through charity work, the early Brothers quickly became politicized. At times they clashed violently with the regimes of Gamal Abdel Nasser and Anwar Sadat until formally renouncing violence in the 1970s. Even so, they continued to be suppressed, suffering jail terms, office raids, and many kinds of discrimination. This only earned them respect and credibility on the Egyptian street. Mubarak painted the Brotherhood as Islamic extremists and the only alternative to his rule—a scarecrow to Egypt's pro-democracy but often Islamophobic allies. Even so, by the late 1990s the group had grown into Egypt's most powerful and popular op-

Amid the feverish atmosphere of the revolution, some Egyptians pause on Feb. 6 to catch up with the news.

position. The Brotherhood won many supporters by providing health and social services to poor Egyptians the government had all but abandoned. Dodging the regime's ban on religious parties, it gained experience in politics by fielding "independent" candidates in parliamentary elections. By the time Mubarak fell, the Brotherhood was primed to become the best-organized political machine in the country.

Keenly aware of the dread they inspired among secular Egyptians and outside Egypt, the Brotherhood trod cautiously: Its political arm, the Freedom and Justice Party, contested only 50% of parliamentary seats and said it would not field a candidate in the presidential election. The Brotherhood also held fast to its pre-revolution rhetoric of being pro-democracy and pro-human rights. The strategy turned out to be a smart one. As the liberals and youth activists fractured and bickered in the chaotic aftermath of the uprising, the Brotherhood kept its eye on the big prize: legitimate power. So when Egyptians voted in the first free and fair elections in the country's history, the Brotherhood secured nearly half of the 498 seats in parliament.

The second-largest number of seats went to a revolutionary wildcard: the ultraconservative Islamists known as Salafis. Previously an almost unknown quantity in Egypt, the rise of the Salafis may have been the Arab Spring's biggest surprise—and according to the liberals, one of its most unsavory fruits. Salafis adhere to a strict and puritanical interpretation of Islam, and were heavily repressed in Mubarak's Egypt, more than even the Brotherhood. Influential Salafists spent years in prison or exile. Many were freed in the general amnesty that followed the dictator's fall. They also enjoyed new freedom to preach and proselytize. Although they had historically criticized democracy as un-Islamic, they quickly embraced the new order and formed political parties. Some Salafis made no bones that democracy was a means to end: the implementation of strict Shari'a, or Islamic law. They won over a fifth of the seats in the new parliament.

In the meantime, Egyptian liberals—including the educated "Facebook Youth" who led the uprising against Mubarak—suffered a backlash from a population desperate to move on from Tah-

The Muslim Brotherhood holds a campaign event in Cairo before the first round of parliamentary elections.

rir. The military and state media vilified the liberals as elite, foreign-funded agents hell-bent on continuing the revolution and fueling instability. Splintered, disorganized, and inexperienced in retail politics, the liberals were unable to fight back. The slogans of the revolution were no match for the argument that Islam was the solution to Egypt's woes—long a motto of the Brotherhood and now adopted by the Salafis too.

After decades in the shadows, political Islam in Egypt has entered a period of renewal. But it was far from clear that the Islamists would be able to hew to their ideology while dealing with the laundry list of challenges facing the country. The Muslim Brotherhood and the Salafis had an uneasy relationship. It remains to be seen whether they can coalesce around a common goal. Far more pragmatic and moderate, the Brotherhood has at times viewed the Salafis as a potential ally, at other times as a troubling and immature force of contention. But Egyptians will measure the Islamists' success in large part on their ability to ensure the country's transition to civilian rule.

Still clutching the reins of power, the stubbornly opaque SCAF showed little intention of handing full authority to an elected government anytime soon. The generals seemed determined to preserve their own political immunity as well as the secrecy surrounding the military's vast economic empire and its network of special clubs, residences, and hospitals—all part of a privileged subculture, impervious to scrutiny, that Mubarak had created to reward a loyal and obedient officer corps. The Islamists faced two unpalatable choices: Risk a possibly violent showdown with the military or make a politically unpopular bargain with the generals.

Perhaps even more daunting was the challenge presented by Egypt's rapidly deteriorating economy. Tourism, one of the pillars of that economy, had yet to rebound from months of civil turmoil, and the Islamists' victory was likely to keep many Western travelers spooked. (It didn't help that some Salafi leaders promised to outlaw consumption of alcohol and to create gender-segregated beaches.) Facing billions of dollars in debt, the transitional government approached the International Monetary Fund for emergency aid in early 2012, but even that seemed unlikely to provide enough relief to keep the country from sliding down a dangerous course.

Given Egypt's strategic importance, its allies and regional neighbors were monitoring its progress carefully. One barometer was the state of religious freedom. The country's Coptic Christian minority—roughly 10% of the population—had already voiced its discontent with the Islamist rise. Copts were institutionally discriminated against under Mubarak, but their condition grew more precarious when sectarian tensions, which had simmered for years, flared with the Salafis' reawakening. After a rash of church burnings and sectarian clashes in 2011, the military crushed a Christian protest in October, killing 25. If the new Islamist-dominated parliament failed to reassure the country's largest religious minority, more violence was inevitable—along with a backlash from the West.

Watching especially closely was Egypt's eastern neighbor, Israel. Egyptian mistrust of the Jewish state has been cultivated by both the Mubarak government and popular culture for years. But since the uprising, leaders ranging from military generals to Salafi sheikhs had raised the tone on anti-Israel rhetoric. In September 2011, protesters stormed and ransacked the Israeli embassy in Cairo. Islamists had promised to rethink and potentially revise the 1978 peace treaty between the two countries, which underpins a complex web of security arrangements throughout the Middle East, as well as long-standing trade agreements. More urgently, Israel feared that an Islamist government might not be inclined to guard its borders as diligently as Mubarak's regime, allowing smugglers to get arms to Hamas in Gaza. Officials from both sides said Bedouin smugglers may have already moved hundreds of surface-to-air missiles from the looted arsenals of Libya's Muammar Gaddafi into Gaza.

The Arab world's largest country faces a difficult and turbulent road ahead, with plenty of potential for violence and further unrest. But there is cause for cautious optimism. Even the most pessimistic Egyptians acknowledge that, with the dictator gone, they at least have a shot at a brighter future. New—if imperfect—political freedoms, combined with economic resources and manpower, could yet add up to stability and progress. And the fact that Egypt remains a strategic hub for the region means that world will not easily let it fail.

Turkey

The Ideal Islamists?

*Led by charismatic Prime Minister Erdogan, the country
is seen as a role model for new democracies and a source
of hope that Islamic politics can be friendly to the West.*

BY BOBBY GHOSH

PRIME MINISTER RECEP TAYYIP ERDOGAN DOMINATES TURKEY'S PO-
litical landscape in a manner not seen since the country's founding father, Mustafa
Kemal Ataturk. The two men would not have gotten along: Ataturk was ferociously
secular; Erdogan is avowedly Islamist. But they have much in common, including
charisma, iron determination, and occasional autocratic impulses. And like Ataturk,
Erdogan's influence extends well beyond the borders of his bicontinental nation.
Since first coming to power in 2002, Erdogan has presided over an economic boom that has trebled
Turkey's per capita income and unleashed entrepreneurship. And, uniquely in the Middle East, he
has done so in a democratic system and for the most part has maintained a pro-West stance. His
people rewarded his Justice and Development Party (known by its Turkish acronym, AKP) with a
landslide victory in 2011's general election, giving Erdogan a third term as prime minister.

Erdogan's rare ability to blend democracy, economic success, and political Islam has made
him a beacon of hope across the Middle East. Opinion polls show he is far and away the most
popular world leader among Arabs. His stock has soared higher still since the Arab Spring. In
countries where young people have risen against old tyrannies, many cite Erdogan as the kind of
leader they'd like to have instead. In the summer of 2011, Erdogan made a sweep through Egypt,
Tunisia, and Libya; everywhere he stopped, he was greeted by crowds as if he were a rock star.

He was hailed, too, at the United Nations General Assembly in New York City, where President Barack Obama, looking past Erdogan's recent trenchant criticism of U.S. policy in the Middle
East, lauded him for showing "great leadership" in the region. The U.S., struggling to come to
grips with the end of old certainties in the region, can only hope that the new governments emerging from the ashes of dictatorships will look a lot like the one Erdogan has built.

For Islamists across the Arab world, Turkey's success is evidence that they can modernize
their countries without breaking away from their religious moorings. Erdogan's Western admirers

Erdogan, greeted with adulation in his travels, won a third term as Prime Minister in a landslide victory in 2011.

see it the other way around: proof that political Islam needn't be an enemy of modernity. It's no coincidence that the Islamist parties that have won pluralities in elections in Egypt, Tunisia, and Morocco have all conspicuously modeled themselves after the AKP.

Erdogan may be the West's idea of the ideal Islamist—conservative yet modern, preachy yet pragmatic—but he's not quite the perfect democrat. He runs roughshod over political rivals, puts enemies in jail, and bullies the media. Many political analysts suspect his plan to rewrite the constitution is designed to amass more executive power. His treatment of Turkey's Kurdish minority has swung from offers of political dialogue to brutal suppression.

And while he may be lionized by new governments in Libya and Egypt, relationships closer to home are not going so well. Erdogan has broken ties with former ally Israel over that country's commando raid on a Turkish-led aid flotilla bound for Gaza. His support for the uprising against Syrian dictator Bashar al-Assad, once a close friend, has taken an economic toll: Syria is a vital trading partner. At the same time, Erdogan's attempts to gain Turkey membership in the European Union have come to naught.

Inevitably, Erdogan's new foreign-policy doctrine, aimed at increasing Turkey's political and economic influence in the Middle East and North Africa, has been dubbed "neo-Ottoman," after the dynasty that ruled much of the Muslim world from Istanbul for 600 years until World War I. Turkish officials envision an arrangement similar to the British Commonwealth, with a constellation of Balkan, Eastern European, and Arab states all looking to Istanbul for benign guidance. But there will be rivals for that role. Iran, Egypt, and Saudi Arabia are the region's traditional powers; there are American and European ambitions too. Relative newcomers China and India have a growing economic interest in the region. While Turkey has a headstart in the Arab Spring countries—it is already one of the largest investors in Egypt and Libya—the competition for influence in the new Middle East emerging from the Arab Spring is bound to be fierce.

One Lens

Award-winning photographer **YURI KOZYREV**
has been covering the Middle East since Sept. 11, 2001.
From Afghanistan to Iraq to the Arab Spring, his camera
has captured the dramatic events that have shaped the
region over the past decade.

Cairo, Tahrir Square
November 2011

Protesters wearing masks
to protect themselves from
tear gas clash with Egyptian
security forces on Mohamed
Mahmoud Street, near
Tahrir Square. After driving
President Hosni Mubarak
from office in the spring,
Egyptians took to the streets
again in the fall to protest
against the military junta,
known as the Supreme
Council of the Armed Forces.

Baghdad, April 2003

Ali Ismail Abbas was 12 when
a U.S. rocket exploding on the
southern outskirts of Baghdad
seared his body and took off both
his arms. When this picture was
taken, he was being tended by
a distant aunt in a Baghdad
hospital, still unaware that the
blast had killed his mother, father,
brother, and 11 other relatives.
Because of Kozyrev's picture
in TIME, Abbas became the
poster child for all wounded
Iraqi children. A charitable
fund set up for him paid for
Abbas to be flown to London
for life-saving treatment.

Ras Lanuf, Libya, March 2011

A rebel fighter carries a load of
rocket-propelled grenades to the
frontline. One month into the
war against Muammar Gaddafi's
regime, the rebels had secured
the eastern cities of Misurata and
Benghazi. It would take seven
more months and thousands of
casualties before the rebels, aided
by NATO air support, were able to
take Tripoli and declare victory.

Cairo, February 2011

First-time protester Fatma Gaber, 16, joins the demonstrations
calling for Mubarak to step down. Rallies against the regime had
been ongoing since Jan. 25, but by February thousands of women
had also joined the crowds in Tahrir Square. "I wanted to join
for Egypt, because I didn't want the people who had died and the
ones who had protested every day to pay the price alone for what
all Egyptians would benefit from," she told TIME. On Feb. 11,
Mubarak resigned, bowing to the pressure of protests that crossed
gender and class lines.

Kabul, May 2009

A group of young boys play in a refugee camp on the outskirts of Kabul for Afghan and Pakistani families displaced by the fighting between U.S.-led forces and the Taliban. According to the U.N., more than 5 million refugees have returned from neighboring countries since 2002, but many live in camps inside the country; more than 80 line the Pakistan-Afghanistan border. Children face a number of threats within the camps, among them smuggling and human trafficking, child labor, and early or forced marriage.

Baghdad, July 4, 2003

Almost five months after the U.S.-led invasion of Iraq, soldiers from the 1st Brigade, 1st Armored Division, 2nd Battalion, 3rd Field Artillery, celebrate the Fourth of July in the palace of Saddam Hussein's son Uday. When they first arrived at the palace, it was filled with pornography, Cuban cigars, and luxury cars, all reflecting the excess of the Hussein family. In following years the area surrounding the palace became a Sunni stronghold and the center of the insurgency.

Downtown Cairo, June 2011

Young Cairenes gather at a café dedicated to Umm Kalthoum, one of the most famous Egyptian singers. The café, near Tahrir Square, represents the heart of revolutionary Cairo, a city that still has more cafés than mosques. Many of the leaders of the protest movement came here to hold meetings during the revolution. Artists, intellectuals, writers, young revolutionaries, and unmarried couples continue to gather to exchange ideas over a coffee or a shared sheesha of flavored tobacco.

Sanaa, Yemen, May 2011

A blind protester attends antigovernment demonstrations
in Change Square. The protests in Yemen started in January
and dragged through the spring and into the summer.
Yemenis came out to protest grievances similar to those
of the rest of the Arab world: corruption, unemployment,
and the lack of political change. After several failed attempts
at a deal brokered by neighboring countries, President
Ali Abdullah Saleh finally signed an agreement in Riyadh
in November to transfer power.

Baghdad, January 2008

Um Seif lost 15 of the men in her family during the Iraq War. Her sons were killed during an American aerial bombing, her husband was shot by an American tank, some have died in prison, others were kidnapped and never returned. During Saddam's regime, Um Seif did not always wear the Muslim veil. She wears one now to mourn the loved ones she has lost.

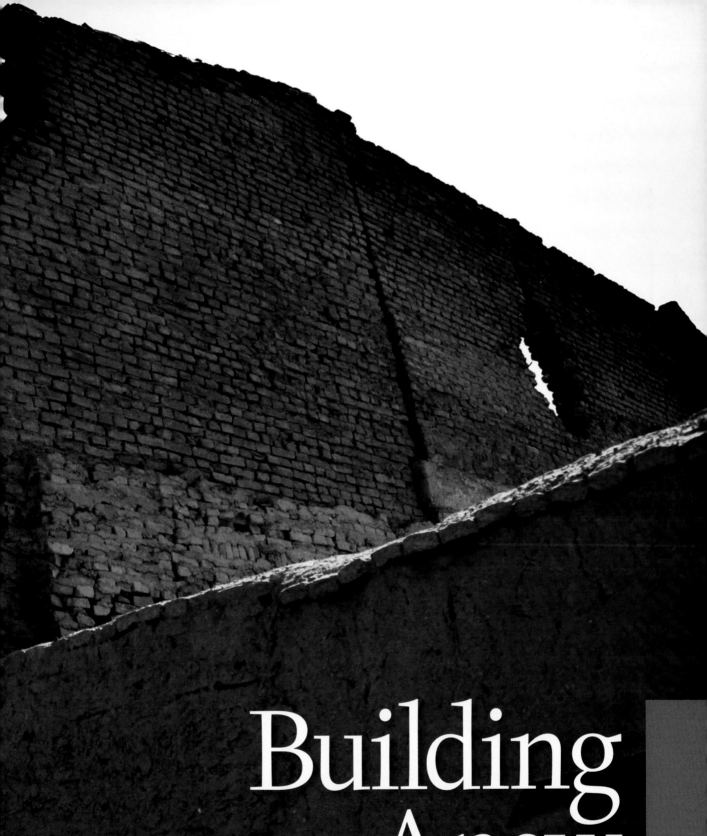

Building Anew

In the war-torn countries of Afghanistan, Iraq, and Libya, fledgling governments struggle to construct new societies and maintain their shaky sense of security. Why their rebirth will be long in the making.

Afghanistan

We Meant Well

*A decade after U.S.-led forces toppled the
Taliban regime, the country is deeply dysfunctional
and faces the prospect of chaos when Western troops
leave. It didn't have to be this way.*

BY ARYN BAKER

O N A BARREN HILLTOP AT THE KABUL MILITARY TRAINING CENTER, Col. Fazl Karim is giving recruits his usual pep talk. In two weeks, when they complete their eight weeks of basic training, they will be commissioned as soldiers in the Afghan National Army. In some ways they look ready: They sit cross-legged in the dirt, aligned in neat rows. The training camp looks functional too. Nearby, construction crews erect more barracks—another 100,000 recruits are expected to go through the U.S.-built training center in the next three years. If all goes as planned, 350,000 men will be ready to defend this country the day the mostly American army of foreign fighters leaves. "You are all going to die one day," shouts Karim. "You might as well die protecting your country!"

Yet they show no particular zeal. A few stifle yawns. Others poke their snoozing companions awake. Even the American officers overseeing all the training are skeptical. Taliban infiltration, drug use, and desertion are commonplace among the men who come here. Troop quality is poor; recruiters can't be too selective when they have such large quotas to fill. U.S. Army Capt. Jason Reed, who is part of the training mission, believes it just needs time. A long time. "As long as training continues when we leave, there is no reason to think that Afghanistan can't continue to grow a professional army," Reed told me. "But it's going to take generations."

The government of Afghanistan and its American patrons do not have generations to make the country work. Afghans are supposed to take responsibility for their own security by Dec. 31, 2014. But 10 years after the U.S. first invaded the country and then settled in for a long occupation, Afghanistan is nowhere close to being able to stand on its own—militarily, economically, or even

PREVIOUS SPREAD: ADEK BERRY/AFP/GETTY IMAGES; RIGHT: YURI KOZYREV/NOOR

Girls attend school in Herat in 2009—a right that had been taken away by the Taliban.

politically. Nevertheless, the U.S. keeps broadcasting its intention to leave—troops, money, and all—as if recoiling from a problem it seemingly no longer has the will or the ability to solve.

That prospect is frightening: Afghanistan today has the potential to be even more destabilizing for the region and the world than it was under the Taliban. Lawlessness has become the rule, so much so that many Afghans have grown nostalgic for the cold but effective dicta of Mullah Omar's Taliban theocracy. Osama bin Laden may be dead and his fraying al Qaeda network dispersed, but once the Americans leave the country, it could easily revert to the failed narco-state and terrorist training ground that it once was. And it risks unleashing another proxy war as rival militias, backed by regional allies, reenact the civil war that saw the rise of the Taliban in the first place.

But American patience for an alternative scenario is nearly tapped out. Over the course of 10 years, more than 1,780 U.S. service members and 760 private contractors were killed and another 14,000 wounded. The U.S. established more than 180 forward operating bases, deployed 9,000 mine-resistant vehicles, and spent nearly $560 billion in the hope of securing and rebuilding the nation. It simply hasn't worked.

At the 10-year anniversary of the 2001 invasion, security was at an all-time low. The U.S. embassy in Kabul endured a prolonged siege, while high-profile assassinations picked off the top tier of government and security officers, including a former president leading peace negotiations with the Taliban. American officials, first in the Bush era and now under President Barack Obama, maintain that economic and security conditions in Afghanistan are improving, but evidence for that claim is scant, even as the deadline for U.S. withdrawal gets closer. In many ways, it has already begun.

When I first came to Afghanistan for TIME in the winter of 2003, I expected resentment, poverty, and destruction. Instead I encountered an extraordinary sense of hope. I ate greasy stews with tribal elders who were expecting roads that would connect their villages for the first time to civilization. I went to school with teenage girls who sat alongside 6-year-olds to get the first-grade education denied to them by the Taliban. I shared the country's dangers too: I was nearly blown up by a suicide bomber and was ambushed alongside U.S. troops near what we had thought was a friendly village. Still, I kept coming back. Like almost all of Afghanistan, I was hooked on hope.

A few years later I moved to Kabul, where I met and eventually married an Afghan-American who had returned after two decades in exile because he, too, believed in the country's future. We had a daughter, and when she was 2 months old, I got her an Afghan passport, determined that she would one day play a part in a resurrected Afghanistan. These days I am starting to think that the flimsy blue booklet, embossed with the Afghan state seal, will be little more than a souvenir of an infancy spent in a collapsed country known best for its drugs, terrorism, and endless history of war.

It wasn't supposed to be this way.

When the U.S. invaded Afghanistan on Oct. 7, 2001, it was with, in the words of President George W. Bush, a moral obligation to "disrupt the use of Afghanistan as a terrorist base of operations" and a promise to raise the hopes of the "oppressed people of Afghanistan." The U.S. toppled the Taliban with little more than a few hundred Special Forces troops on horseback and satchels full of cash. Yet the enemy who seemed defeated simply melted into the population while its leadership plotted a return from safe havens across the border in Pakistan. As the U.S. became distracted by the Iraq war, the Taliban slipped back into Afghanistan, laying the groundwork for a tenacious insurgency. At the same time, the U.S. spent tens of billions on instant-gratification projects lacking long-term impact. Roads crumbled within years of completion, a result of poor-quality materials brought in by shady subcontractors. Security contractors paid bribes to the Taliban to stop them from attacking fuel convoys. In a country without wheelchairs, medical clinics came equipped with handicap ramps. Schools were built, but no teacher-training colleges were established to staff them.

By some measures, Afghanistan has made progress. Twice as many Afghans have electricity now as in 2001. Many have better access to basic health care. American assistance has helped boost the attendance in elementary and secondary schools for girls from nearly nothing in 2001 to more than 3 million; for boys, from 1 million to over 5 million. Nothing makes me happier than seeing the streets of my neighborhood swarming with girls in white head scarves making their way to class. They want to grow up to be president, they tell me, or doctors or pilots so they can see the world.

Yet it is all undermined by the lack of security. As attacks on the capital have increased, the economy has nosedived. Foreign and private investment has stalled. "Our economy depends on security," says Mohammad Azim, who runs an international cash-transfer office in Kabul. "When there is no security, everyone sends their money abroad. So business is good for me but bad for Afghanistan." It will get worse, he says, the closer it gets to 2014. When the foreign forces depart, the support industries, from private security to trucking and construction, will collapse, Afghans fear.

The U.S. ambassador, Ryan Crocker, called the August 2011 terrorist attack on the embassy "harassment," but his glib assessment did little to reassure Afghans after the deftly planned assault paralyzed the capital for 19 hours, took 16 lives, and demonstrated the militants' ability to penetrate the most heavily guarded areas of the city. Not long after the attack I got an e-mail from my local assistant, who was in Sweden for a three-month fellowship, telling me he wasn't coming back. A bright, energetic law student who speaks English using slang learned from American troops, Shah often voiced his dreams of making a difference for his country. No longer.

The conspicuous training of Afghan soldiers offers scant comfort. A fundamental pillar of the American exit strategy is the assumption that the Afghan army will be able to stand up as Americans withdraw. Afghans make good soldiers, and brave ones, but as Capt. Reed pointed out, the timeline of their readiness extends far beyond America's deadline to leave. In September the Pentagon halved its budget for the next three years of training, paying, and equipping the Afghan national security forces. A possible reduction in the already low salaries—about $200 a month for an Afghan army private—could lead to wider defections. One soldier, picking up his salary at Kabul's money-changing market, looked doubtfully at the wad of cash in his hand when asked what he would do if his pay were cut. "I'd quit," he said simply. Another soldier said he would probably join the Taliban. He was only half-joking. "I hear they pay better."

U.S. attempts to rapidly boost the number of alternate security forces may be undermining stability. A report released by Human Rights Watch documents alarming levels of abuse by the Afghan Local Police, a force created by the U.S. in remote areas where more formal security forces are spread thin. These militias have been accused of rape, murder, extortion, armed land grabs, and in one gruesome case, hammering nails through the foot of a suspected teenage insurgent.

President Obama's decision to increase U.S. troops in Afghanistan by 30,000, to a total of 100,000, has failed to defeat the Taliban insurgency and in some ways has backfired. The military situation in the south has improved but remains shaky in the eastern and northern sectors—and in some provinces has deteriorated. The Taliban have shown a capacity for daring raids—for example, springing more than 600 detainees through an underground tunnel out of a prison near Kandahar. At the same time, the increase in air strikes and night raids that harm innocents along with insurgents are starting to undercut public support for the foreign forces. "We don't want the foreigners to leave," says human rights activist Shoukria Haider. "We know they are the only thing standing between us and a return to civil war. But the longer [they] stay, the more violence we see, so we are caught. We want the violence to end too."

Based on recent history, it's easy to say that Afghanistan is ungovernable and impervious to modernization. But before the 1980 Soviet invasion, my mother-in-law wore Chanel suits and held

a senior position in the national airline. My father-in-law worked for a functioning government that was slowly bringing the country development and progress. Even today my Afghan friends run successful media companies and work in a vibrant telecommunications sector. Yes, they are urban exceptions in a country whose rural population is still mired in poverty, but their success points to Afghanistan's possibilities if the country were given the tools it needs.

But instead of building a Marshall Plan showcase, the U.S. came up with a patchwork of short-term solutions that seem designed to give the appearance of progress rather than create enduring change. More damaging, perhaps, is that the U.S. has cynically looked the other way when Afghan government officials, whose salaries are paid by American funds, flagrantly indulge in corruption and graft. Afghans are equally at fault. Police take petty bribes, power brokers rape with impunity, and parliamentarians steal land. The lawlessness has many Afghans nostalgic for the era when a single Talib in the town square would dispense justice with a quote from the Koran and the bite of his lash. The sister of an 11-year-old rape victim whose politically connected attacker was never prosecuted once shouted at me with rage and frustration, "If the Taliban were still here, that rapist would have already been executed by now." Few Afghans, however, support the wanton violence of the reincarnated Taliban insurgency. The hope that government talks with the insurgents in 2011 would bring peace evaporated when a Taliban peace envoy detonated his explosives-stuffed turban while embracing the leader of the National Reconciliation Council. Burhanuddin Rabbani was killed instantly in a clear demonstration of what the Taliban truly feel about making peace: They don't need to compromise. They just need to wait.

A poppy worker inside the former compound of Mullah Omar, the spiritual leader of the Taliban

Police train in the province of Herat in November 2011 (top), but the shattered windows of a Kabul shopping center (bottom) reflect the Taliban's ability to intimidate the civilian population with terrorist attacks.

Nearly nine years after I set my first, nervous foot on Afghan soil, my battered Nokia flashlight phone (essential in a country where power outages are common) is stuffed with the numbers of now departed diplomats, soldiers, press officers, consultants, and development experts. I, too, am only a temporary visitor these days—my husband and I moved a year and a half ago, when we reluctantly came to the conclusion that our beloved city wasn't safe enough to raise our child. Each time I return, I find that the barricades are bigger, the garlands of razor wire more numerous. Anxiety and fear nibble on the edges of conversations. Many Afghans have an exit strategy as well.

Military officials say that things will get worse before they get better and that it will take time for the shaky Afghan forces to find their footing. Meanwhile the Taliban have taken their campaign of rural intimidation to the cities, where their highly organized suicide attacks undermine whatever confidence is left. NATO officials blithely assert that suicide attacks are a sign of desperation, proof that the enemy is no longer capable of mounting a frontal attack. Perhaps, but the Taliban's ability to recruit "martyrs," as demonstrated by their use of three or four at a time, suggests a far more terrifying kind of strength. While U.S. diplomats and military officials in Kabul weave a hopeful narrative of progress, few of us on the ground see it that way. It used to be that American withdrawal was conditioned on success. Now, it seems, withdrawal has become the definition of success. If that's the case, America's mission to build a country will feel a lot like failure. —*With reporting by Massimo Calabresi in Washington, D.C., and Walid Fazly in Kabul*

Iraq

What War Has Wrought

As U.S. troops departed, sectarian violence flared anew. Now the ravaged country faces the daunting task of healing itself.

BY BOBBY GHOSH

I N THE EARLY HOURS OF DEC. 18, 2011, A CONVOY CARRYING 500 American soldiers rumbled across the border into Kuwait, marking the formal end of the U.S. occupation of Iraq. Half a world away, President Barack Obama sought to portray the withdrawal as a political promise kept: He had vowed to bring the troops back home, and now he had done so. He left out the fact that he had wanted to maintain a significant military presence in the country but had been thwarted by Iraqi politicians, who refused to give the soldiers immunity from local law. No matter: Most Americans were relieved to see the end of a foreign misadventure that had lasted more than seven years, took nearly 4,500 American lives, and—depending on which economist you believe—cost anywhere from $800 billion to $3 trillion.

Iraqis were doing some math too. While the absence of reliable record-keeping meant it was impossible to know exactly how many Iraqis had been killed during the 2003 war and the years of violence that followed, some studies put the toll at 100,000, others at six times that number. The economic cost was even harder to calculate, but certainly devastating. Most Iraqis were glad to see the last of the U.S. military, and Prime Minister Nouri al-Maliki basked in the moment as if he were a triumphant general. "It is Iraq's day," he said in a New Year's Eve TV address. "It is the dawn of a new day in Mesopotamia...Your country is free."

American soldiers board a C130 at Baghdad Airport during the U.S. pullout from Iraq in December 2011.

Life goes on: A vendor sells snacks in Baghdad a week after the American military exited his country in December 2011.

Maliki's bravado struck a discordant note with many Iraqis as well as Americans. Mesopotamia's "new day" seemed a lot like the old one: reddened with blood. The start of the post-American era was heralded by a series of bomb blasts in major cities that brought the country to the precipice of a new sectarian war. Corrupt and inefficient, Maliki's government gave little comfort to Iraqis and even less reassurance to foreigners. Iraq was still showing the scars of war, physical, sociological, and psychological. In the end, there was little discussion in either country about the reasons the war had been fought. It was no longer necessary to point out that Saddam Hussein had possessed no weapons of mass destruction and was not supporting al Qaeda. Nor had the introduction of democracy in Iraq changed the Middle East: The Arab Spring had sprung up on its own.

If there is consensus that the war was fought for the wrong causes, there is also a general acceptance that some of its consequences were nonetheless beneficial. Americans and the majority of Iraqis can agree that the toppling of Saddam Hussein and the dismantling of his brutal regime were positive outcomes. And the war, for all its imperfections, did lead to democracy. As a result of these achievements, Iraqis now enjoy freedoms that were unthinkable in the Saddam era.

Historians will long debate the cost both countries paid for those achievements. But the outcomes of war are not static. The cost-benefit calculus can change with time. If things turn sour in Iraq, if the country disintegrates amid sectarian and ethnic violence, if its democracy fails, then the enormous sacrifices made by Iraqis and Americans will have been wasted. But if Iraq can evolve into a state at peace with itself and its neighbors, if it can live up to its vast economic potential, the moral of the story will be seen quite differently.

Which outcome is more likely? The early omens were gloomy. Within 24 hours of the U.S. withdrawal, Maliki had roiled sectarian tensions by ordering the arrest of Vice President Tariq al-Hashimi for allegedly abetting terrorists, which sent him fleeing to the autonomous Kurdish region in the north. Maliki is Shi'ite Muslim, as are 60% of Iraqis; Hashimi is Sunni Muslim, a member of the minority that has long made up the country's ruling elite. Democracy has given Shi'ites power, along with the opportunity to wreak vengeance for hundreds of years of Sunni oppression. The two communities were caught up in a brutal civil war, fought by armed militias, that peaked in 2006–07. The "surge" of additional U.S. troops helped restore calm, but there has been no process of reconciliation between the sects, and many of the militias remain at large, ready to respond to any perceived provocation—like the arrest warrant against the country's top Sunni politician.

A campaign of bomb attacks followed, most of them against Shi'ite targets. The frequency and frightening efficiency of the attacks were reminiscent of the worst months of 2006–07. Shi'ite militias have refrained from open retaliation, but that may be merely a matter of time. In Sunni neighborhoods of Baghdad, many are arming to protect themselves from a counterattack.

Renewed violence will frighten away many investors, local and foreign. In the two years leading up to the U.S. troop withdrawal, Iraq saw something of an economic upswing. New shops and businesses were popping up in Baghdad streets, construction projects were creating jobs, and the oil sector was drawing investment after decades of neglect. And it's not just foreign investors who are spooked. Perhaps more damaging to the country's economic potential, the chronic violence and Maliki's political belligerence will keep refugees from returning home. More than 1 million Iraqis who fled the country during the sectarian bloodbath of 2006–07 still live in Arab states like Syria and Jordan. Those refugees tend to be educated and affluent, and they represent the bulk of Iraq's intellectual capital. Many are doctors, engineers, architects, business managers—exactly the kind of people the country needs to rebuild its war-shattered infrastructure and mismanaged economy. But most of the refugees are Sunnis. Maliki's pursuit of Hashimi will make many wonder how they themselves would be treated if they went back home.

Nor is Maliki necessarily winning points with his own sect: Muqtada al-Sadr, the radical Shi'ite cleric and a key member of Maliki's ruling coalition, has called for fresh elections. Shi'ite businessmen who have gained from recent economic growth fear they may lose everything if sectarian violence continues. Young Shi'ites worry more about jobs (youth unemployment is believed to exceed 30%) than about taking revenge on Sunnis for historical wrongs. In the face of Sunni-Shi'ite violence, investment will tend to detour to the Kurds, an ethnic minority that enjoys a great deal of autonomy in the oil-rich northern provinces. They have long enjoyed the fruits of political stability in their domain: Foreign investors seeking a foothold in Iraq are more likely than not to start in the north.

The toppling of Saddam has created space for one other player in Iraq: its neighbor Iran. Indeed, commentators in the West and in Arab states speculate that the departure of U.S. troops will allow Shi'ite Iran to extend its influence over Iraq. But these fears may be overblown. Iraqis, Shi'ite and Sunni alike, have historically viewed Iran with suspicion. The ethnic divide between the two countries—Iranians are Persian, most Iraqis are Arab—cannot easily be bridged by shared sectarian beliefs. Geography dictates that Iran and Iraq will seek to influence each other and trade with each other. But Iraq seems no more likely to become a puppet of Tehran than of Washington.

What influence, if any, will the U.S. have in Iraq's future? It will certainly have sizable diplomatic clout: The largest American embassy in the world is in Baghdad. Washington will also have a seat at the Baghdad political table in the name of the Kurds, who have long enjoyed close relations with the U.S. The ties between the Pentagon and the U.S.-trained Iraqi military will only be strengthened by future arms sales. There will be other business deals too. As it rebuilds, Iraq will need help in everything from pumping and refining oil to creating fast-food restaurants. American businesses will compete for some of that action, and they may not get any special consideration for the fact that the U.S. spent vast amounts of blood and money to make such competition possible. But that, too, is a positive outcome of the Iraq war.

Libya

The Rebels as Rulers

Ridding themselves of Muammar Gaddafi was an astonishing achievement for Libya's rebels. Now they face the mighty challenge of rebuilding their oil-rich but poorly run nation.

BY VIVIENNE WALT

Y U R I   K O Z Y R E V / N O O R

MUAMMAR GADDAFI'S VIOLENT DEMISE IN October 2011 after 42 years in power left Libya's new leaders with the task of rebuilding a country almost from scratch. Far different from Tunisia and Egypt, Libya had had no semblance of modern government for two generations. There was no parliament, no political parties, and few ministries. All had been declared by Gaddafi in the Green Book, his manifesto, to be corrupt systems that favored the rich. Now the Green Book has been replaced with a clean slate, which in many respects could be a virtue.

By 2011, Gaddafi's autocracy had become unbearably suffocating to most Libyans. The country was no longer the backward desert nation of his early revolution. Half the population was younger than 24, most people lived in cities, and most had known only Gaddafi's rule. When Western companies began constructing office towers and luxury hotels after foreign sanctions ended in the mid-2000s, Libyans believed that their country was on the cusp of change. Instead, Gaddafi refused to yield an inch of power. And yet, despite Gaddafi's tight control of media, by 2011 it had become almost impossible to stifle political thought. The explosive popularity of satellite television gave Libyans a close-up look into life elsewhere, including the rest of Africa, where millions of people much poorer than themselves

Rebels flee Gaddafi's army in March 2011; that month the U.N. demanded a cease-fire and declared Libya a no-fly zone.

were voting in multiparty elections. With frustrations at a boiling point, the Egyptian and Tunisian revolutions gave many Libyans the sense that their dictator, too, could be overthrown. His defeat exacted a heavy toll, however. The grueling eight-month war killed about 14,000 Libyans, many of them students and professionals who had rushed into battle with little preparation. When the rebels finally cornered Gaddafi and killed him, few—even among his close associates—mourned.

Having won an astonishing victory, Libya's politicians had little time to celebrate. The most urgent problem was the mountain of weaponry now in the grip of the militias who had fought the war. Hundreds of thousands of AK-47s were stashed in civilian homes. Gaddafi had splurged on arms purchases and left huge caches—at one location more than 5,000 shoulder-fired missiles.

That arsenal provides ample potential for bloodshed should Libya split into factions. For the interim leaders, an immediate task was to try to heal the fissures between regional tribes and ethnic groups, whom Gaddafi had long pitted against one another. So the administration, the National Transitional Council, promised to locate the critical Oil Ministry to Benghazi, the revolution's birthplace; the Finance Ministry in the city of Misurata, where a brutal wartime siege had

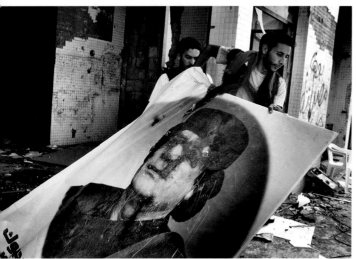

Libyans discard one of the ubiquitous Gaddafi images.

Libya retains massive reserves of oil and natural gas.

killed about 2,000 people; and the Culture Ministry in the far-eastern town of Darna. The scheme seemed unworkable for a modern state, designed instead to reward those who had led the revolution and to trumpet a clean break from Gaddafi, who ran Libya from his Tripoli fortress like a medieval monarch, neglecting millions in the heartland.

The greatest potential for violence lies in Libya's newest schism: between technocrat politicians, many returned from decades in exile, and members of the new militia, who bore the brunt of the fighting. In December 2011, shortly after the installation of a new prime minister (himself a returnee from the U.S.), fighters from the tiny western town of Zintan, who led the August assault on Tripoli, battled the nascent national army for control of Tripoli's airport. Thousands of Libyans poured into Martyrs' Square, demanding that the militia disarm and leave Tripoli. The commanders ignored the call. The revolution was over, but the scramble for power was just beginning.

The thrill of liberation is yielding to the grind of governing and rebuilding. Libyans are digging out not only from a dictatorship, but from a war that ravaged entire neighborhoods and halted economic activity for nearly a year. The leaders will need also to create a thriving middle class, since thousands left Libya during the 1970s and 1980s after Gaddafi nationalized businesses and properties without compensation. Even when privatization began in Gaddafi's later years, few Libyans risked making major investments, fearing that they could lose it all again.

Libya's new leaders have one huge advantage: natural wealth. With just 6.5 million people, the country sits atop mammoth reserves of 47 billion barrels of oil and about 1.5 trillion cubic meters of natural gas. Even if the economy fails to diversify, those resources could generate income for decades. There is cash aplenty too. The interim administration began work with $180 billion in foreign-exchange reserves left over from Gaddafi. Unlike Tunisian President Zine El Abidine Ben Ali or Egyptian President Hosni Mubarak, Gaddafi did not stash billions in secret accounts for his personal use, perhaps because he had vowed to die in Libya or because he could not imagine being ousted.

How best to harness that wealth? One important task is to overhaul the country's schools, since Libyans will need an intensive catching-up period to compete globally. In 2004 the World Economic Forum's Global Competitiveness Report ranked Libya's educational system, with its overcrowded, dysfunctional schools, at the bottom among 111 countries. At that time, Libya had more teachers per student than Sweden or the U.S., but a third of them never showed up for work.

Libya's new government will also need to generate millions of jobs if it wants to avoid being voted out of office by those finally free to fire their leaders. By 2011, Libyans were entering the job market with few useful skills, according to corporate executives, who report having to train new recruits in the basic work ethic. Unemployment is around 30%, though even that high figure understates the problem, since tens of thousands of Libyans work in poorly paid government posts, contributing little to the economy.

One reason for optimism is Libya's fresh leadership. Since Gaddafi's regime was totally smashed, the chances of a pro-Gaddafi insurgency spreading widely, as it did in Iraq after Saddam Hussein's collapse, seems slim. The sole high-profile Gaddafi figure left alive in Libya is his once-powerful son Saif al-Islam, whom Western leaders ironically had hoped would reform Libya, and who awaits trial and possibly execution.

Among Libya's new leaders, the interim council contains several people who dreamed for years about how to remake Libya, and who have spent time drafting post-war plans. They will need to think on their feet as well: Within weeks of the council starting work, Libyan workers struck for higher wages, while in Benghazi thousands more demonstrated for a more transparent administration.

Besides its oil reserves and cash on hand, Libya has a lot of advantages that could be leveraged to build a new nation. One is location. The world's largest market, the European Union, is a mere two-hour flight from Tripoli. Hundreds of miles of Mediterranean coastline dotted with spectacular Roman ruins could be the basis for Libya's first tourism industry. And with the vastest desert on earth, Libya seems ideally suited for giant solar farms similar to those in next-door Algeria, with the potential to sell electricity to energy-hungry Europe. Consultants have advised Libyan politicians that simply by investing $15 billion or so, the country could also begin making refined petroleum products rather than only shipping crude oil. That would greatly expand energy revenue and create thousands of new jobs.

When 2011 began, Libyans could scarcely imagine being able to debate how to transform the country. Such talk would have invited arrest or even death at the hands of Gaddafi's security forces. But as 2011 came to an end, Gaddafi had been reduced to a reviled figure of history, whose clownish image is spray-painted in graffiti across the country; on one downtown wall in Tripoli the wild-haired leader is depicted being exterminated with a can of insecticide. Having strutted for decades as an egomaniacal autocrat, Gaddafi is yesterday's man. Now Libyans need to create their own tomorrow.

Women on the March

To a surprising degree, the revolution has been female-powered. In a region known for unequal rights, women demonstrated not just to claim a voice for citizens but also to start liberating their own gender.

Yemeni activist Tawakkul Karman was named one of three winners of 2011's Nobel Peace Prize.

Saudi Arabia

Driving for Change

*In one of the most unexpected revolts of the
Arab Spring, Saudi women defied the country's ban
on women driving. Is it a path to greater freedoms?*

BY ARYN BAKER

I N MAY 2011, A JERKY, LOW-QUALITY VIDEO OF A WOMAN DRIVING A CAR became an international YouTube sensation, garnering nearly 100,000 views within a week of being posted. Why? Because the woman, Manal al-Sharif, a Saudi divorced mother of two, was breaking the law of her country in the most public way possible: by posting the act online. Saudi Arabia is the only country in the world where women are not allowed to drive. And al-Sharif's video, before Saudi authorities blocked it, was a call to arms. During the nine-minute-long video, in which she drives past the strip malls and shopping centers emblematic of modern Saudi life, al-Sharif describes the absurdities of living in a country that professes to honor women so much that it doesn't allow them to drive. "They tell you that you are a queen, that you are protected, a jewel," she says. "But it is humiliating." The assumption is that every woman has a man to look after her. The reality is that husbands and fathers and brothers die or divorce or go abroad to work. Or simply don't have the time to act as chauffeurs. "You will find a woman with a Ph.D., and she doesn't know how to drive," says al-Sharif. "We want change in the country."

In one of the most peculiar revolts to have been inspired by the Arab uprisings, al-Sharif proposed a day of protest in which women would take to the streets—not on foot, but behind the wheel. They were to leave their drivers at home and head out on their own to the grocery store or to the doctor or to pick up their kids from school. Those thankless errands may plague women around the world, but for some in Saudi Arabia they are a long-dreamed-of freedom.

Al-Sharif was detained for her defiance and eventually apologized for her acts in a public confession on national TV, but the movement had already taken root. Across Saudi Arabia more women posted videos online of themselves driving, and on June 17, 2011, scores of women risked

PRECEDING PAGES: LUKE SOMERS/DEMOTIX/CORBIS; RIGHT: LYNSEY ADDARIO/VII

A woman in Riyadh joins a day of protest on June 17, 2011, by getting behind the wheel and going for a drive.

arrest by taking the driver's seat. It was the first significant challenge in decades to the harsh rules governing Saudi women, and while the law still has not changed, the movement represents a hairline fracture in the fortress that has kept Saudi women from exercising basic human rights.

Maha al-Qatani, a petite woman with a merry smile that masks an iron will, was one of the women who went out on June 17. She went prepared, her Coach bag stuffed with a toothbrush, deodorant, a change of clothes, and a prayer rug—all the essentials for a possible prison stay. Detention for a Saudi woman isn't just an inconvenience; it is a black mark on her reputation and a smear against her whole family. Still, al-Qatani, like al-Sharif, was willing to risk it. "If no one sacrifices, no one will get their rights," al-Qatani told me as I accompanied her on her maiden drive. We had just pulled onto one of Riyadh's broad boulevards when a phalanx of police cruisers forced us to the side of the road. Al-Qatani had hoped that a publicized prison stay would bring more attention to the cause; instead all she got was a yellow slip of paper. Al-Qatani stared at it for a moment, her brow furrowed in confusion. Then she broke into peals of laughter. "It's a ticket," she shouted, pumping her fist. "Write this down. I am the first Saudi woman to get a traffic ticket." For anyone else, a traffic ticket is nothing but a headache. For al-Qatani it was a badge of honor, proving that she had defied a prohibition on women driving in the kingdom and, she hopes, paving the way for more women to do the same.

Saudi Arabia, with its vast, unpopulated deserts, low-slung architecture, and cheap oil, is a country made for cars. The capital, Riyadh, is bigger than Los Angeles and has no public transportation system. But to many women the prohibition against driving is merely the inconvenient symbol

Until early 2011, Saudi curbs on working women meant only a man could sell lingerie; now only a woman may.

of greater limitations on women's lives in the kingdom. "Driving is a stand-in for everything else," says influential women's rights blogger Eman al-Nafjan. "As a woman, I am discriminated against in every single aspect of my rights as a citizen." Saudi women now cannot leave the country without permission from a male guardian. They cannot take out loans without having two men vouch for their identity, even if they carry government-issued IDs. Custody laws automatically favor the father. If women are allowed to break the driving barrier, says al-Nafjan, "everything else is possible."

It's not just the activists who know this, but conservative clerics as well. What looks like progress to some resembles chaos to the religious leaders who dominate Saudi society. "As long as women aren't driving, the religious establishment feels secure," says al-Nafjan. That is why something as simple as driving has inflamed tensions across the kingdom.

Driving per se is not really at issue. At least two of the Prophet Muhammad's wives are known to have ridden camels, and one led the prophet's followers into battle on horseback. It's what driving brings that causes consternation. "There is nothing in the Koran that prohibits a woman from driving," admits Sheikh Abdallah al-Oweardi, a self-described moderate religious scholar. But in religious rulings, conservative clerics have argued that driving allows women too much freedom and might lead to illicit mixing of the sexes. To the religious council that advises the Saudi monarchy, women driving is the first sign of the apocalypse. A recent study conducted by a religious scholar and endorsed by the council frets that if women are allowed to drive, in 10 years there will be no virgins left in the kingdom. Driving might not be mentioned in religious texts, but there are several references to the societal risks of women and men being alone together. The

At a resort near Jeddah, Saudi youths can frolic in mixed company; the religious police generally don't go to the beach.

draconian-seeming laws exist, says al-Oweardi, "to protect our women from harassment and to protect society from the problems you see in the West—single mothers and illegitimate children—that come from unconditional relations between men and women." When I asked him what a conservative religious scholar would tell me, he laughed and said that one would never speak with a female journalist.

In many matters regarding women, Saudi Arabia differs little from Afghanistan under the Taliban. The main difference is that the desert kingdom has enough money to ensure equitable treatment in terms of health care and education. Separate but equal is not an epithet in Saudi Arabia; it is the goal. In September 2011 the government opened the doors to one of the country's most ambitious projects to date—a 2,000-acre women's university, complete with dorms to house 12,000 students, 14 colleges, a teaching hospital, an Olympic-caliber athletic stadium, and a mosque big enough for 5,000 worshipers. It is quite literally a world of women. The $5.3 billion campus was constructed in such a way that all maintenance can be conducted via underground tunnels, ensuring that no man will ever need to set foot on university grounds. Women will staff cleaning crews, as well as the army of gardeners needed to tend the spacious lawns and floral borders. Female attendants will manage the integrated monorail system, though in order to adhere to the ban on women drivers, the system itself is automated.

In a nation that takes the segregation of the sexes seriously, the investment and planning that have gone into ensuring that this world of women stays untainted by a male presence (there are male professors, but they teach via video link) has been widely welcomed. Still, some Saudis wonder if it hasn't gone too far. The constant preoccupation with separating men and women, says architect Nadia Bakhurji, has become a drain on resources. "I sometimes wonder if that time and effort and money could be better spent on medical research, or better hospitals, or improving our education system."

Quite possibly. But for the moment, the new university answers an increasing demand for women's education—58% of all university students are female, a stark change from the 1960s, when girls were not educated at all. That achievement is not matched in the workplace, where women account for less than 15% of the labor force, mostly in the education and medical sectors. The predominance of educated women is setting Saudi society up for far more difficult questions to come: Where will those women work when they graduate?

The government is urging private businesses to hire more women—under conditions designed to prevent mixing between unrelated men and women—but it is hard to see how that will happen if they can't drive to work. Many middle-class families see little incentive to let their daughters and wives work if they end up spending their salaries on drivers. Architect Bakhurji estimates that she spends an extra 25% in overhead just providing cars and drivers for the female staff at her firm. It's a sacrifice she is willing to make, she says, but in most other businesses, "it becomes a barrier to hiring women." Eventually, she argues, the sheer numbers of educated women will force change in the archaic laws that govern the kingdom, and while she wants the laws to change sooner rather than later, she is not so sure that the Arab Spring protests will bring the change many women want to see.

In fact, while the women's campaign to drive may have friends abroad, in Saudi Arabia it has proved deeply divisive. Women's rights activists are conflicted over the impact of acts of civil disobedience in a society uncomfortable not only with dissent but also with women in the public eye. This year's protests are not the first. In 1990, 47 women drove through Riyadh in a formal demonstration. They were all arrested, they all lost their jobs, and they—and their husbands—were barred for a year from leaving the kingdom. To this day the Drivers, as they are known, face discrimination. Some argue that the protest set the women's movement back, forcing the clergy to issue religious rulings condemning driving that were then codified into government edicts.

The modern nation of Saudi Arabia has emerged only recently from an intensely conservative Bedouin culture that traditionally kept female family members concealed within the home. When the country started urbanizing in the 1960s, women adapted by wearing the face-covering niqab in public. While more liberal women may now show their faces, the majority of the population continues to cover up out of modesty. So the sight of Saudi women on YouTube has been too much for some to bear. "This kind of activity is not part of our culture," says al-Oweardi. Many Saudi women whose families are wealthy enough to afford drivers don't see driving as a priority. "We are our own worst enemy in terms of emancipation," says Riam Darwish, who works for a popular religious-affairs television program. She supports women's right to drive but says she won't join the protest. "If I get caught, it could harm my family. I have too much to lose." Paradoxically, the women who would benefit the most from being able to drive are members of the more conservative lower classes. "The actual change in driving will have to come from the women who can't afford drivers," says Darwish. "But they are the ones who believe that women shouldn't drive."

The king, for his part, has declared driving by women a "social" issue and has said it is up to the public to decide what to do about it. But there is no clarity on how the public could do so: While municipal councils are now elected (women will be able to vote for the first time in 2015), there is no space for Saudis to weigh in on national issues like driving. Some right-to-drive campaigners, fearing that the majority is against the idea, would rather see a royal decree like the one the king's half-brother King Faisal issued in the 1960s declaring that girls could go to school. The ruling family gets its legitimacy from conservative clerics, who follow a strict interpretation of Islam. Pushing too forcibly for change could backfire, causing instability at exactly the moment the Saudi succession is at its most fragile. King Abdullah is 87, and the royals most likely to be next in line are equally aged. Some observers say King Abdullah is waiting for the succession to stabilize before he tackles a subject considered toxic to conservative clerics.

Conservatives and campaigners for the right to drive would at least agree on this: Allowing women to drive is about more than getting from point A to point B. It's a symbol of more profound changes that could fundamentally alter Saudi society. For conservatives, who believe it is ordained by God that women stay in the home and take care of the family, it means a loss of control over women's lives. For some women's rights campaigners, driving is a stepping-stone to other freedoms. "Driving means access, mobility, and empowerment, and from there we can chip away at the bigger issues," says Fawzia al-Bakr, one of the original Drivers in 1990.

Not all activists agree. "The domino effect doesn't work in Saudi Arabia," says activist Muna Abu Sulayman. She fears that allowing women to drive would simply become a sop to the demands of Western governments and Saudi liberals without fundamentally altering women's role in society. "You have to wonder, What's the point of being able to drive if you can't leave the country on your own? Women in many instances are treated like second-class citizens, children almost. All these core issues have to be dealt with first. And if we check the driving box off, they won't be."

A better solution, says Najla Hariri, an unassuming housewife in Jeddah, is not to make a fuss. Her husband, a pilot, is often away. And if the family driver doesn't turn up for work, she takes the car keys. She doesn't see herself as particularly heroic. "I am just a mother taking my kids to school. I am not trying to challenge the government," she says with a shrug. "I just got tired of waiting."

Social change, Hariri seems to be saying, doesn't always have to come from campaigns or conflict. Sometimes it creeps in when one woman decides to do something without asking for permission. Or when another gets a traffic ticket instead of a prison sentence.

All in the Eyes

In Saudi Arabia eye makeup is an especially important aspect of a woman's style, since it's the only part of the body visible to the public.

A Sense of Style

Westerners visiting the Middle East are often surprised by the kaleidoscope of women's fashions they encounter. Here's a sampling of the region's increasingly varied styles.

BY CLEO BROCK-ABRAHAM

Royal Couture

Queen Rania of Jordan, the glamorous wife of King Abdullah II, is frequently ranked among the world's best-dressed women. She favors designer labels like Lanvin, Dior, and Elie Saab.

Traditional Flair

Top right: Women in the countryside in Iran wear the burqa, a loose body covering, and a colorful niqab, which covers their eyes.

Total Coverage

Bottom right: These Afghani women in the market in Kunduz wear the chadri, which is similar to the burqa but has a net or grille over the eyes. It was mandatory during the Taliban era but is now only loosely enforced by local warlords.

Wedding Chic
Married to Prince al-Waleed Bin Talal, the billionaire investor, Princess Ameerah al-Taweel of Saudi Arabia often flouts the very religious country's sartorial traditions. At the royal wedding in London in April 2011, she wore custom-made couture by Zuhair Murad, a Lebanese designer.

CLOCKWISE FROM LEFT: JASPER JUINEN/GETTY IMAGES; ANWAR AMRO/AFP/GETTY IMAGES; KHALED DESOUKI/AFP/GETTY IMAGES; SAMUEL ARANDA/CORBIS; IAN LANGSDON/POOL/AGP/CORBIS

Culture Shock Haifa Wehbe of Lebanon (top left) is considered one of the sexiest women in the Middle East, known as much for her scandalous outfits as for her pop music.

Subtle Differences Above, top: several versions of the hijab, or Islamic head scarf, in Egypt. The woman in the middle sports the two-piece al-amira hijab. She's flanked by women in the shayla hijab, more like a shawl or wrap with loose folds.

Defiantly Dressed Above, bottom: Women in Tunisia joining the Arab Spring protests often turned hijabs into revolutionary bandanas.

High Fashion The chic wife of the Emir of Qatar, Sheikha Mozah (left, in berry), is adept at marrying designer styles with conservative Islamic dress codes. Here her hijab is styled like a turban.

69

In Gaza militant culture is being displaced by politics, but factionalism has often diffused the Palestinian message. Here, a young Palestinian boy carries a toy gun.

A Matter of Identity

As Arab liberation sprang forth, Israel carried on as if little had changed, focusing inward as Palestinians clamored ever louder for statehood and increasingly brought the global community to their cause.

A "separation barrier" has helped remove the threat of Palestinian terrorist attacks, allowing Israelis to relax.

Israel

Splendid Isolation

What Arab Spring? While the rest of the Middle East was shaken and stirred by revolution and regime change, Israelis worried about food prices—and took time to catch some rays.

BY KARL VICK

THE ARAB SPRING MAY HAVE TRANSFORMED THE world beyond Israel's borders, turning the security assumptions of the region's lone superpower into a kaleidoscope, every successful revolution shifting the outlook until the next one, when everything shifted again. But at bottom, the events of 2011 underscored the defiant isolation Israel already had embraced on its own. Nothing that happened outside Israel challenged the prevailing preoccupation inside the Jewish state, which remained Israel itself. If anything, events abroad reinforced the home truth that, with the possible exception of the U.S., no one else could be trusted—and so energy was best directed where it generated a reward, in the domestic realm. It says volumes about Israel today that most of its residents would remember 2011 not for the Arab Spring but for the summer of tent protests that prefigured the Occupy movement. Except that the Israeli version proved far more successful than its U.S. equivalent, bringing hundreds of thousands of middle-class citizens into the streets to march for a more equitable distribution of income.

"Israel has no foreign policy," Henry Kissinger famously said, "only a domestic political system." It's not just the politicians who are insular. Pollsters describe Israelis as markedly uninvolved in foreign affairs, including anything having to do with the perhaps 4 million Palestinians living literally on their doorstep. The fences that ring much of the West Bank and Gaza keep Palestinians largely out of sight, and increasingly out of mind. Surveys have shown that fewer than one in 10 Israelis regard the conflict over territory with the Palestinians as the "most urgent" concern. There's some anxiety about the missiles fired over the fence by militants in Gaza and the possibility of a nuclear-armed Iran. But poll after poll shows Israelis as among the happiest in the world.

And why not? In the four years since the last suicide bombing on their soil, Israelis have found a chance to enjoy themselves. On the eastern shore of the Mediterranean the sun strikes skin at an angle that, on a good day, erases the possibility that anything can matter except this sky, that sea, and the land between. No city in Israel is more than 40 minutes from the beach, and for all the talk of settlements, three out of four Israelis choose to live on the coastal plain. The immediate question is how to make the good life better. Founded by socialists, the country's late embrace of capitalism had produced divisive wealth: a gap between rich and poor exceeded by only four other countries in the OECD, none founded on Israel's collective ideal.

So it was that in February 2011, as Cairo's Tahrir Square filled with revolutionaries, ordinary Israelis calculated the consequences of unfolding events on two levels. Paramount, as always, were the security implications. Egypt has been the linchpin to Israel's defense architecture since 1979, when President Anwar Sadat signed a treaty that essentially ended the likelihood of conventional war. In the three decades since, Israel's defense budget went from 25% of GDP to 7%. The treaty paved the way for the 1994 pact with the Hashemite Kingdom of Jordan that secured Israel's other long flank, to the east. Signed at the White House, both pacts were backed by the full faith and credit of the U.S., which like Israel put "stability" and nonaggression toward the Jewish state ahead of persistent questions about human rights and fair elections in the Arab world. The Egyptian despot Hosni Mubarak shared Israel's distrust of both Iran and the political Islam championed by the Muslim Brotherhood, progenitor of Hamas. Jerusalem was alarmed to see him go. If much of the world swelled with inspiration at the power of people who simply gathered in one place and chanted slogans, Israelis fretted over how easily a crowd could become a mob.

As the Arab Spring flowered, Israel lay low, gratified that the protesters railing against Mubarak, Libya's Muammar Gaddafi, and other Arab tyrants didn't so much as mention either Palestine or the Jewish state: One analyst compared the Arab Spring to the Copernican revolution, upending the idea that the world revolved around Israel. But by autumn a genuine mob had overrun Israel's Cairo embassy. Salafists, an Islamist group that makes the Brotherhood seem practically godless in comparison, made a strong showing in Egypt's parliamentary elections. Missiles looted from Gaddafi's arsenals showed up in Gaza. And the Sinai peninsula, which Israel surrendered for peace in 1979, became a lawless staging ground for terror attacks from groups inspired by al Qaeda.

There was more. In Jordan, the monarchy on which Israel had placed a huge bet was feeling the breeze from the Arab Spring: A suddenly attentive King Abdullah twice fired his entire cabinet in a show of responsiveness to public opinion. On the West Bank the most moderate Palestinian leadership in history had not only given up on moribund peace talks and shifted its hopes to the United Nations, but was also moving—under pressure from a youth movement—to reconcile with archrival Hamas. For Israel, only events in Syria offered positive possibilities: The decline of President Bashar al-Assad carried grave implications for Hezbollah, the Shi'ite militia that had gathered 45,000 missiles from its godfathers in Tehran, delivered to Lebanon by way of Syria.

It was amid this tumult that Prime Minister Benjamin Netanyahu chose to alienate Israel's closest Muslim ally, Turkey, by refusing to apologize for the deaths of nine Turks at the hands of Israeli commandos a year earlier off the Gaza coast. The Flotilla Fiasco illustrated the inversion of

Israeli Prime Minister Netanyahu with President Obama at the White House in the spring of 2011

Israel's international image – from David, knocking down invading Arab armies in its first decades of existence, to Goliath, the regional superpower that seemed incapable of anything but a military approach to any problem.

But if it was a failure of diplomacy, it carried no evident consequences for Netanyahu. By the time Ankara recalled its ambassador, the Likud leader had demonstrated mastery of the only alliance that mattered. In Washington, Netanyahu publicly lectured President Barack Obama on how he ought to conduct his foreign policy in the Middle East, then basked in 29 standing ovations from a joint session of Congress, where Christian Evangelical support has made Israel an apple pie issue.

No less important, the prime minister expertly survived the Tent Protest that dominated Israel's summer. It was a nearly spontaneous camp-in that turned a posh Tel Aviv street into a communal happening. Begun to protest the lack of affordable housing, the movement expanded to exuberant marches of 350,000 people under the broader demand of social justice. In the end, no one was entirely certain what that specifically meant. The protests largely ignored the towering structural challenges of the Israeli economy, the fastest-growing segments of which—Ultra-Orthodox men and Arab women—tend not to seek employment. But afterward Israelis said they felt closer to one another, united, for a change, by something besides apprehension.

Palestine

Road to Recognition

*A flailing attempt to gain formal statehood
in the United Nations was, in the end, a distraction
from political challenges closer to home.
Will the real Palestine please stand up?*

BY KARL VICK

PALESTINIANS WILL SOMETIMES BOAST OF INTRODUCING DEMOC-racy to the Arab world. It's not a specious claim: From the Israeli prisons where 40% of Palestinian men spend at least a portion of their lives and choose leaders by ballot, to the polling stations where voting is monitored by international observers in the Gaza Strip and West Bank, electioneering has gone on long enough to qualify as a tradition. But it's one easily overlooked in a nation more readily defined by what it lacks—sovereign borders, political unity, and both the trappings and reality of statehood.

Six decades after rejecting the 1947 U.N. resolution proposing to divide between Jews and Arabs the scoop of land from the Jordan River to the Mediterranean Sea—choosing instead to confront the nascent Israel militarily and catastrophically—the descendants of the Arabs who then lived on the disputed land remain dispersed, and not only geographically. Divided by faction, ambition, and the question of how to deal with Israel, the one thing they agree on is that they are "Palestinians." For a national identity forged in the crucible of dispossession, exile, and defeat, the name resonates so powerfully and persistently around the globe as to constitute a brand. More than 120 nations recognize Palestine as a state, and when a formal application for U.N. membership was submitted to the General Assembly in September 2011, the response was roaring ovations. But within weeks the application drifted into the wishful uncertainty that has defined Palestinian national aspiration.

Consider the credentials of the man hoisting the application into the air from the podium. Mahmoud Abbas has at least three titles. As head of the Fatah Party, he leads the secular faction

Demonstrators in a West Bank village walk past spent tear-gas grenades as they protest against Israeli settlements.

Fishermen prepare to cast off from Gaza City: Israel permits them to operate only within three miles of shore.

that gave rise to Palestinian nationalism when it was formed in the 1960s around the charismatic militant Yasser Arafat. Abbas also chairs the Palestine Liberation Organization, the umbrella group representing Palestinians the world over and signatory to all agreements, such as the 1993 Oslo Accords with Israel. It was Oslo that mandated the other organization Abbas heads, the Palestinian National Authority, to govern Palestinians in the West Bank and Gaza Strip.

In fact, however, for the past five years the PA's writ has extended only to the West Bank, home to perhaps 2 million residents. The government of the 1.6 million Palestinians some 20 miles away in Gaza was in the hands of the Islamic Resistance Movement, known as Hamas. That militant religious group, an offshoot of the Muslim Brotherhood, won parliamentary elections in 2006 and pushed Abbas's Fatah out of the coastal strip a year later. The division expressed the duality always at play in the Palestinian public—negotiation or resistance, or some combination thereof. Palestinians say they will find the balance themselves, but their first priority is unity, a goal made elusive not only by politics but by geography. At least as many Palestinians live outside the Occupied Territories, in the surrounding nations to which their parents or grandparents or, in some cases, they themselves fled in 1948 or in the Six Day War of 1967, when Arab armies set out to undo Israel and instead lost swaths of land to the superior Jewish army. Some 400,000 now live in Lebanon, another half million in Syria. And about 2 million moved west to Jordan, where most were given citizenship after that country annexed the West Bank (only to lose it in the Six Day War). Not that you have to live abroad to be a refugee. About 800,000 residents of the West Bank and more than 1 million Gazans live in camps, which over the decades have come to resemble ramshackle cities.

Also often regarded as Palestinian are about 1.5 million residents of Israel descended from the Arabs who remained in their homes in 1948 and became citizens of Israel, sometimes referred to as Israeli Arabs. There's also the Palestinian diaspora, a million or more who reside in Europe, the Americas, or elsewhere in the Middle East.

All in all, it makes for a delicate patchwork sort of nation, but one sustained by international sympathy as well as funds. Israeli legal experts complain that Palestinians are unique in being allowed to pass on the status of refugee from generation to generation. They argue that the situation in the region's 56 refugee camps nourishes the notion that Palestinians will one day return to their homes in land that has been Israel for six decades. And indeed the "right of return" remains a Palestinian rallying cry that does more to stir passion than prepare the population for the compromises that would come with any negotiated settlement.

The layers of aggrievement also pose a challenge for Palestinian leaders grappling for an effective way forward. Twice Palestinians launched uprisings, or intifadehs, against the Israeli occupation. The first, in the late 1980s, was characterized by young men facing down tanks with slingshots. It cemented the Palestinian role as underdog, reversing the historical dynamic of the conflict that cast tiny Israel against the entire Arab nation. It also proved to be the preamble to Oslo, the treaty with Israel that was supposed to end with a Palestinian state. Oslo and more was undone, however, by the Second Intifadeh, which was characterized by suicide bombings. Begun in 2000, the uprising cast the Palestinians as terrorists, especially among an American population that after 9/11 came to identify with Israel more than ever. By the time it was over, at mid-decade, the "Separation Barrier" was going up around land Israel wanted to keep, the Palestinian economy was in tatters, Arafat was dead, and the public appetite for resistance was at a nadir. Abbas, long the PLO's most persistent advocate of nonviolence, handily won election as president, calling for a negotiated end to the occupation.

But duality again: When Israel pulled its settlements and troops out of Gaza in 2005, Hamas claimed credit, arguing that violent resistance had carried the day. Emboldened by its victory in the legislative elections, the group launched wave upon wave of missiles into Israeli territory until the Israel Defense Forces launched a crushing military operation for three weeks bridging 2008 and 2009. Israel brushed aside criticism of the death toll (1,400, half of them civilians) and of the siege it continued to enforce, keeping out all but essential foods and medicines until 2010, when outrage over civilian deaths in a bungled commando raid on a Turkish aid ship forced a reappraisal.

The challenge emerging on the West Bank was to show the world that Palestinians could govern themselves. Under Abbas and his prime minister, Salam Fayyad, a technocrat with excellent relations with Western powers, the West Bank government set out to fulfill the requirements of statehood. With money and training from the U.S. and the European Union, smartly uniformed troops enforced Fayyad's policy of "one law, one gun." The relative quiet paid dividends both for Israel and for Fayyad's government. Western donors contributed billions of dollars to Fayyad's campaign to establish the building blocks of a viable state. Tens of thousands of pubic employees came to rely on foreign aid for their salaries.

This fiscal reality tempered the Palestinian bid for statehood. Because Israel opposed the U.N. application, the pliant U.S. Congress voted to cut aid if the Palestinians pressed for membership in any U.N. agencies beyond Unesco, which welcomed Palestine with great fanfare in October 2011. In response, Abbas shifted toward internal affairs, specifically the delicate business of reconciling with Hamas. Among Palestinians, the rapprochement was the most visible outcome of the Arab Spring, emboldening masses to insist that their leaders unite against the larger enemy that was the occupation. And on March 15, 2011, when thousands of young people went into the streets in Ramallah and Gaza City, Hamas and Fatah first tried to suppress the protests, then sent their own faithful into the throngs, shouting in favor of reconciliation as if it had been their idea in the first place. It took nine months for the factions to agree who should lead a unity government: Abbas (giving him yet another title). But, being Palestinian, there was quick consensus on what should come next—new elections.

Dangerous Places

In the midst of the upwellings of democracy, a growing antagonism toward the West radiated from Pakistan and Iran, one of them with nuclear weapons and the other allegedly with ambitions to join the club.

In Pakistan gunmen on motorbikes set ablaze at least 19 fuel tankers on their way to supply NATO forces in Afghanistan.

Pakistan

A Bad Marriage

A rogue military, weak political leadership, unchecked terrorist groups, and a rising anti-American tide—for all that, the U.S. needs its dysfunctional relationship with Pakistan to work.

BY ARYN BAKER

PRECEDING PAGES AND THIS PAGE: BANARAS KHAN/AFP/GETTY IMAGES

WHEN THE U.S. CONFRONTED PAKISTAN after the terrorist attacks of Sept. 11, 2001, there were no discussions of common goals and shared dreams. There was just a very direct threat: You're either with us or against us. Pakistan had to choose between making an enemy of the U.S. and a quick and dirty deal sweetened with the promise of cash for the trouble. In the end, Pakistan's cooperation in the Bush administration's "war on terror" was a transaction that satisfied the urgent needs of the day, brokered by a nervous military dictator, Pervez Musharraf, who failed to explain the deal to his people. That allowed a theme to become fixed among Pakistanis: The war on terror was America's war. When Pakistani soldiers started dying in battles against militant groups, when suicide bombers began killing Pakistani civilians, it was America's fault, because it was America's war.

So when the biggest success in America's war culminated in a midnight strike on a compound deep in the heart of Pakistan's military establishment, killing Osama bin Laden, many Pakistanis concluded that they had been betrayed by their supposed ally. How dare the Americans sneak into their country without so much as a warning and conduct a military operation just 75 miles from the capital? They also felt betrayed by their own

Supporters of a pro-Taliban party shout anti-U.S. slogans at a protest in Quetta after the killing of Osama bin Laden.

At a parade in Islamabad, a missile-laden truck passes the portrait of Pakistan's founder, Mohammad Ali Jinnah.

military. How could it be that Pakistan's armed forces, which claim a lion's share of government spending, were clueless about the presence, a mere mile from its most prestigious defense academy, of the world's most wanted terrorist? Cyril Almeida, one of Pakistan's best-known columnists, summed up the national anguish in a column: "If we didn't know [bin Laden was in Abbottabad], we are a failed state; if we did know, we are a rogue state."

Pakistan is a bit of both. The military controls foreign policy, national security, and an intelligence network so pervasive that no dinner guest at a foreign journalist's house goes unscrutinized. The civilian government, hobbled by incompetence and corruption, has no power and, worse, no backbone. In tea shops and on street corners, Pakistanis' frustration with their leaders collides with their inability to change it. Instead they lash out at the U.S. for holding up a mirror to their own failure as a nation.

During a parliamentary address in which he was expected to account for the security lapse that allowed bin Laden to hide for five years in Abbottabad, Prime Minister Yousuf Raza Gillani chose instead to lambast the U.S., accusing it of violating the country's sovereignty and warning that Pakistan had the right to retaliate with "full force" against any future strikes. "Let no one draw any wrong conclusions. Any attack against Pakistan's strategic assets either overt or covert will find a matching response." He insinuated that the U.S.-Pakistani relationship was on the rocks. Others were more blunt: "To hell with the Americans," said retired Brig. Gen. Shaukat Qadir, a regular guest on television talk shows. "We need to reconsider our relationship."

A similar sentiment can be heard in the halls of Congress, where many are demanding to know why we have given more than $20 billion in U.S. aid over the past decade to a country that shelters and arms our enemies even as it purports to hunt them down. "I think this is a moment when we need to look each other in the eye and decide, Are we real allies? Are we going to work together?" said U.S. Speaker of the House John Boehner.

It's not just the rhetoric that's heating up: Each side seems eager to poke the other in the eye. The U.S. has launched drone strikes at several sites in Pakistan since the Abbottabad operation, knowing full well they will infuriate the Pakistani military, which sees them as an invasion of sovereignty. And Pakistan-based terror groups, such as the virulently anti-American Haqqani Network, thought to be behind a 17-hour assault on the U.S. embassy in Kabul in September 2011, has been able to continue its anti-NATO operations unmolested by Pakistan's security agencies. The outgoing chairman of the Joint Chiefs of Staff, Adm. Michael Mullen, in his final appearance before the Senate Armed Services Committee, said, "The Haqqani Network acts as a veritable arm of Pakistan's Inter-Services Intelligence agency"—Pakistan's military intelligence wing.

The troubled relationship hit a new nadir in November 2011, when NATO forces in Afghanistan responded to a cross-border attack and mistakenly killed 24 Pakistani soldiers under murky circumstances that have inflamed tensions on both sides. Yet for all the anger in Islamabad and Washington, neither nation has much choice. However duplicitous, however volatile, the U.S.-Pakistani relationship is central to the interests of both countries. The U.S. needs Pakistan's help to be successful in Afghanistan—it provides, among other things, a vital transit link for goods destined for coalition troops in the landlocked country. But regardless of Afghanistan, the U.S. needs Pakistan to be stable. The alternative—a collapsing nation awash with terrorist groups and a nuclear arsenal—is too awful to consider. How real is that prospect? "Pakistan is passing through one of the most dangerous periods of instability in its history," warns Anthony Cordesman of the Center for Strategic and International Studies. "[It] is approaching a perfect storm of threats, including rising extremism, a failing economy, chronic underdevelopment, and an intensifying war, resulting in unprecedented political, economic, and social turmoil." That alone is enough to challenge any thoughts of cutting it loose. Throw in the fact that it also has nuclear weapons and has in the past sold plans to the highest bidders under circumstances that may or may not implicate the army, and you start to get a picture of a country whose collapse could easily take the region with it. Pakistan is simply too nuclear to fail.

The relationship, in truth, has never been about trust. It was, and is, a strategic alliance founded on complementary interests: Pakistan's desire for military assistance and fear of becoming a pariah state, and the U.S. need for regional support in the Afghanistan war. While Pakistan and the U.S. share similar long-term goals—economic partnership, stability in the region—their short-term needs rarely intersect. That is why the question of whose side Pakistan is on is so galling to most Pakistanis and so infuriating to most Americans. "Pakistan is on Pakistan's side," says former Sen. Tariq Azim.

Carved from the newly independent India in 1947, Pakistan has never fully resolved the quandary with which its founder, Mohammed Ali Jinnah, wrestled: Is it a Muslim state or a state for Muslims? While his Indian counterpart, Jawaharlal Nehru, ruled for nearly two decades, long enough to realize his vision of a secular state, Jinnah died a year after Pakistan's founding. A succession of weak civilian governments and military dictatorships followed. In that period India and Pakistan fought three wars, mainly over the contested territory of Kashmir. In 1971, Indian military support for separatists in East Pakistan led to the creation of Bangladesh. That humiliation informs Pakistan's actions still and its belief that India constitutes an existential threat capable of destabilizing and further dismembering Pakistan. That fear of India, in turn, explains Islamabad's quest for nuclear weapons, which was realized in 1998.

For the first three decades of Pakistan's existence, its leaders, both military and civilian, ran a largely secular state. That changed in 1977, when Gen. Zia ul-Haq took power in a military coup. He cemented his rule by instituting Islamic law and revising the educational curriculum in an effort to promote nationalism and an Islamic identity. Had it not been for the 1979 Soviet invasion of neighboring Afghanistan, Pakistan's secular elite might have rebelled. Instead the country rallied in support of its neighbor, out of fear that it might be next. Fearing the same thing, the U.S. supported Pakistan as it armed and trained Afghan mujahedin to take on the Soviets. This required both subterfuge and a certain amount of denial: Since U.S. law forbade aid to a nation pursuing nuclear weapons, Washington pretended Pakistan was doing no such thing. When Soviet forces pulled out of Afghanistan in 1989, Pakistan was left with more than 3 million Afghan refugees and a generation brought up with the culture of jihad. Then, in 1990, Pakistan's nuclear program was finally recognized, and the U.S., which had already cut aid, imposed sanctions on Islamabad. "You used us, and then you dumped us," says Qadir, the retired general, echoing national sentiment. "And Pakistanis are convinced you are going to do it again."

The U.S.-Pakistan alliance in the 1980s vastly empowered the Pakistani military and the ISI. American aid flowed through them, swelling their sense that they alone could safeguard the nation's interests. When Pakistan returned to civilian rule in 1988, the military retained effective control of national security and foreign policy, redirecting Islamist fervor against India in a protracted guerrilla war. Civilian rule lasted barely a decade. By the end of 1999, Musharraf, another general, had seized power in a coup. The U.S. didn't seem that concerned. After 9/11, sanctions were lifted and aid restarted, with the Pakistani military again serving as the main conduit. In exchange, Islamabad would enable the free flow of supplies to NATO troops in Afghanistan, allow covert U.S. operations against terrorist groups sheltered in Pakistan, and mop up any groups that threatened U.S. interests. Musharraf's replacement by a civilian government in 2008 didn't change the terms of the deal, but it coincided with growing concern in the U.S. that the Pakistanis were not keeping up their end of the bargain. While Pakistan was indeed doing battle against some terrorist groups, it also seemed to allow others to thrive.

The bargain struck in 2001 seems to have broken down. Many Pakistanis would like that, if it meant Washington would now work with their democratic institutions instead of the military. But they know from history not to hold their breath. For the past two decades Pakistan's military has engaged in a campaign of divide and conquer, setting political parties at odds and preventing the emergence of a strong civilian government. It has bought media complicity—either through intimidation or by threatening to cut out lucrative advertising from military-owned enterprises. Even if the raid in Abbottabad has taken some of the shine off the military brass, the generals can be relied upon to stoke anti-American sentiment as a diversion. The military is adept at making even good news look bad. In the autumn of 2009, when the civilian government cheered the prospect of U.S. legislation tripling nonmilitary aid, the generals stepped in to denounce its conditions as humiliating. The Kerry-Lugar bill marked the first time Washington had addressed the dire socioeconomic problems of Pakistan and the need to reinforce democracy, but the military rightly perceived as a threat a rider stipulating that funds would cease in the event of a coup.

Meanwhile, little has been done to take on militants in North Waziristan, a haven for the Haqqani Network. To retired ambassador Tanvir Khan, who served in Afghanistan in the 1980s, the cost of taking on the Haqqanis would be too high for Pakistan to bear. You have to pick your battles, he says. "If the army does in North Waziristan what the Americans want it to do, overnight the Haqqanis become enemies of Pakistan."

Nevertheless, the awkward truth remains: The U.S. needs Pakistan. American officials be-

Policemen stand guard at the site of a suicide car bombing in Karachi; eight people, including three cops, were killed.

lieve that bin Laden's death offers an opportunity to peel the Taliban away from al Qaeda. And when that happens, Pakistan will be perfectly poised to offer its assistance. Though routinely denied by Pakistani officials, it is hardly a secret that Taliban leader Mullah Mohammed Omar has been using Pakistan as a base of operations ever since he fled the U.S. invasion in 2001. With the target date for turning over responsibility for Afghan security to the Afghan army by the end of 2014 approaching, there is nearly universal agreement that the Taliban will have to be involved in some sort of political reconciliation.

So for Washington, says Sen. Azim, the question boils down to this: "A decision has to be made. Can you use Pakistan, with all its warts? My submission is that you don't have anyone else, so you might as well use us. Not by twisting our arm or accusing us. You know, do it nicely by sitting down with us and listening to our point of view. Our objective is to have a friendly government in Afghanistan. Americans want a safe, honorable exit. Let us help you."

It may appear perverse to attempt to expand a relationship with a country so seemingly disposed to working against American interests, but the reality is that an unstable, friendless, and nuclear-armed Pakistan would be an even greater threat. If it isn't already, Pakistan has the potential to quickly become the most dangerous country in the world. It could collapse. A jihadist coup would put weapons of mass destruction in the hands of people who would not hesitate to use them. Or the country could launch a nuclear war with India. Adm. Mullen may have been openly disgusted with Pakistan's perfidy, but even he recognizes the need to strengthen the bonds. "Now is not the time to disengage from Pakistan; we must, instead, reframe our relationship," he said in the same parting address in which he attacked the ISI. "A flawed and strained engagement with Pakistan is better than disengagement." It may have been inadvertent, but he appeared to be invoking an old saying as popular in the Pakistani tribal areas as in Hollywood: Keep your friends close, and your enemies closer.

Iran

Nuclear Nuisance

*Facing international isolation and
crippling economic sanctions, the Islamic republic
is backed into a corner. That makes it an
unpredictable actor in an unstable region.*

BY ISHAAN THAROOR

IRAN HAS ALWAYS BEEN AN OUTLIER IN THE MIDDLE EAST. A NON-ARAB nation with no history of Ottoman rule, it boasts a distinct and proud cultural legacy and stands at a remove from the vicissitudes of politics in the Arab world. Well before the 1979 revolution and the advent of the country's distinct brand of religious nationalism, popular sentiment was tinged with a historical chauvinism. Iranians are the heirs to centuries-old dynasties and empires, and the memory of that former grandeur still echoes in the grandstanding of the current Iranian leadership. No surprise, then, that the geopolitical ambitions of the Islamic republic seem as outsized and overreaching as the presumed mandate of the revolutionary theocratic state. Like the Safavid potentates 500 years before them, the mullahs in Tehran harbor visions of regional domination.

For years, the 1979 revolution gave the regime an element of street cred in the Arab world. Tehran unabashedly championed an emancipatory, anti-Western populism, rhetoric that appealed to those chafing under the yolk of dictatorships or repressive monarchies backed by the U.S. and other NATO powers. But the upheavals of 2011 have shown that Arabs don't need Iran's help, or even its example, to get rid of their dictators. And while the Arab street may have little interest in aligning itself with Washington's vision of the world, it's none too keen on playing into Tehran's hands either.

So the Iranians have focused on building up a level of strategic, asymmetric power in the Middle East that is neither "hard" nor all that "soft." With ties to a host of rogue militant outfits in the region, Iran's elite and secretive Revolutionary Guards maintain a level of strategic depth there. In recent decades U.S. officials have spied the hand of the Guards—specifically, the Quds Force, its foreign wing—in terrorist plots from Latin America to Saudi Arabia. The Guards have ties to the Shi'ite group Hezbollah in Lebanon and the Islamist group Hamas in the Occupied Territories. Iran has also maintained strong relations with the Ba'athist regime in Syria, a vital conduit of aid

President Mahmoud Ahmadinejad visits a nuclear-enrichment facility in the central Iranian city of Natanz.

and arms to Hezbollah. In Iraq the 2003 U.S. invasion that ousted the Sunni Ba'athist dictator Saddam Hussein arguably worked in Iran's favor; Iraq's current Shi'ite-dominated government in power has strong links with Tehran.

Aside from Arab paranoia over an Iranian-sponsored "Shi'ite crescent" arching from the Caspian Sea to the Mediterranean, the greatest threat emanating from Iran in recent years has been its steady, clandestine advances toward possessing nuclear weapons. A report issued in the fall of 2011 by the IAEA, the U.N.'s nuclear agency, alleged for the first time that Tehran had designs on procuring or assembling the bomb; the Iranians, including their vitriol-spewing president, Mahmoud Ahmadinejad, claim their efforts to enrich uranium and expand nuclear facilities are for purely civilian purposes. But there is growing fear that Iran could, in the near future, launch a missile bearing a nuclear device at Israel, the state at which Ahmadinejad directs his most hateful rhetoric.

In response, the U.S. and other Western nations have stepped up new rounds of sanctions on the already alienated Iranian regime. Foreign intelligence agencies, chiefly Israel's Mossad, may also be behind a campaign of covert ops and sabotage that has claimed the lives of key nuclear scientists and damaged strategic military facilities. It's unclear whether such tactics alone can contain Iran: Even liberal Iranians who oppose the Ahmadinejad regime back the country's nuclear ambitions, and Tehran can still count on the tacit support of Russia and China, a significant importer of Iranian oil, on the U.N. Security Council. More direct confrontation, through aggressive military posturing and diplomatic brinkmanship, may only strengthen a regime that has long made political hay out of the threat of Western meddling. Iran cuts a complex geopolitical pose, and its shadow falls over many corners of the Middle East. But its domestic politics are similarly complex, riven by factions and power struggles, with a recently quieted pro-democracy movement still capable of rising up once more. It may be those internal dynamics, rather than the often unsuccessful attempts of an embattled regime to project its power abroad, that determine Iran's fate.

Adrère Amellal, Siwa Oasis, Egypt.
Sitting near the edge of Siwa Lake, this
eco-lodge is built in the traditional way,
from mud, and decorated with the work of
local artisans. The hotel has no electricity,
so rooms are lit with beeswax candles.

Rising From the Desert

Modernity meets tradition as new skyscrapers, eco-friendly hotels, and houses of worship create innovative skylines across the region. In this portfolio of striking designs, history's influence is rarely predictable.

BY CLEO BROCK-ABRAHAM

Yesil Vadi Mosque, Istanbul

Referencing the circular shape of the Ottoman mosques, the architect Adnan Kazmaoglu blends tradition and innovation in a building the *New York Times* called "austerely geometric." Fulfilling the role of the mosque as a central place in Muslim society, the structure includes a meeting hall, a library, activity rooms, and a courtyard.

Yas Viceroy Hotel, Abu Dhabi
Top left: The first hotel in the world built over a Formula 1 race circuit, the Yas Viceroy breaks boundaries. Its signature design feature: an LED-illuminated canopy.

Royal Opera House, Muscat, Oman
Above: Built by order of Oman's ruler, Sultan Qaboos, the new opera house incorporates traditional forms of columns and terraces to create a modern Omani design.

American University in Cairo, New Cairo
Left: A $400 million campus was erected on 260 acres in a Cairo suburb, drawing on classical Egyptian architecture to create a sense of place.

The Dubai Mall, Dubai
Below: The biggest mall in the world features a 10 million–liter aquarium and an Olympic-size skating rink.

The Museum of Islamic Art, Doha, Qatar

Architect I.M. Pei hoped to capture the "essence of Islamic architecture" in his design for the museum (left). The end product is a bold structure with sharp geometric lines that will house a collection of Islamic art from the 7th to 19th centuries.

Burj Khalifa, Dubai

Standing at 2,716.5 feet, the Burj Khalifa is the tallest building and tallest free-standing structure in the world. It is home to corporate offices, residences, and the Armani Hotel. The surpassing structure also shared the screen in 2011 with Tom Cruise in *Mission Impossible: Ghost Protocol*.

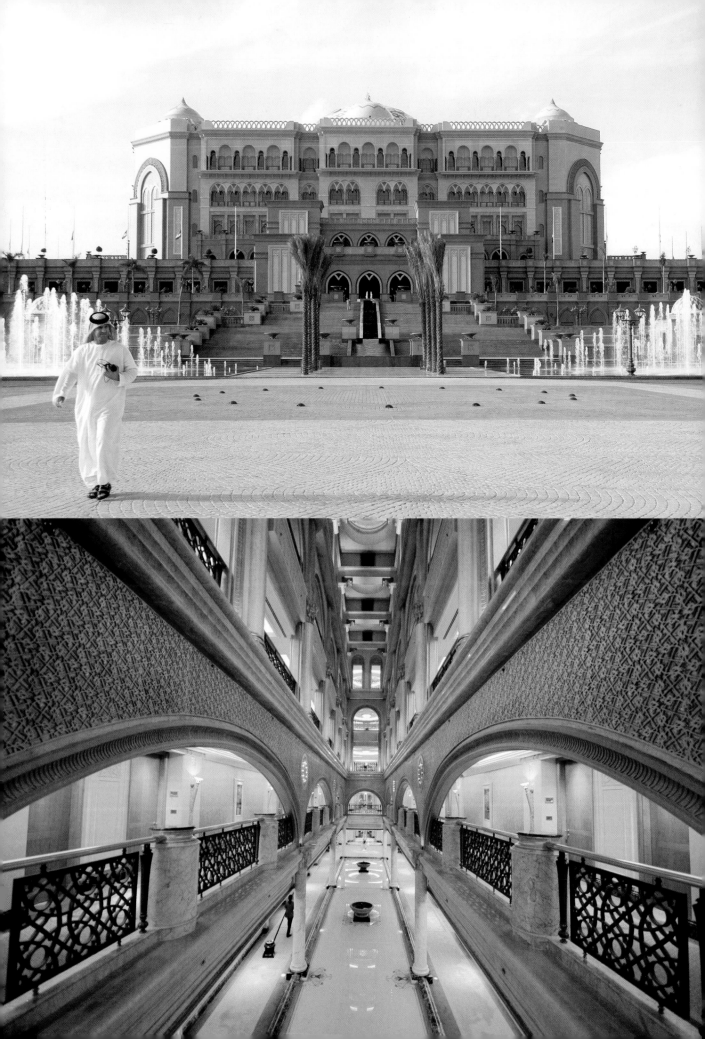

Emirates Palace, Abu Dhabi

Far left: This $3 billion hotel is the second most expensive ever built. Designed for luxury on a regal scale, the structure contains 114 domes, more than 1,000 chandeliers, 394 rooms and suites furnished in gold and marble, as well as 40 conference rooms and a helipad.

Doha Skyline, Qatar

Above: Doha, the capital of Qatar, has seen explosive population growth during the past decade. As the economy diversifies from its original economic base in oil and natural gas, skyscraper construction is booming. The teapot monument is one of the few nods to tradition.

Abraj Al Bait Towers, Mecca, Saudi Arabia

Left: With the tallest clock tower in the world as its centerpiece, this complex overlooks Islam's holiest site, the Masjid al-Haram, which is the destination of the Hajj (the Muslim pilgrimage). The building houses a hotel, a shopping mall, and residential towers.

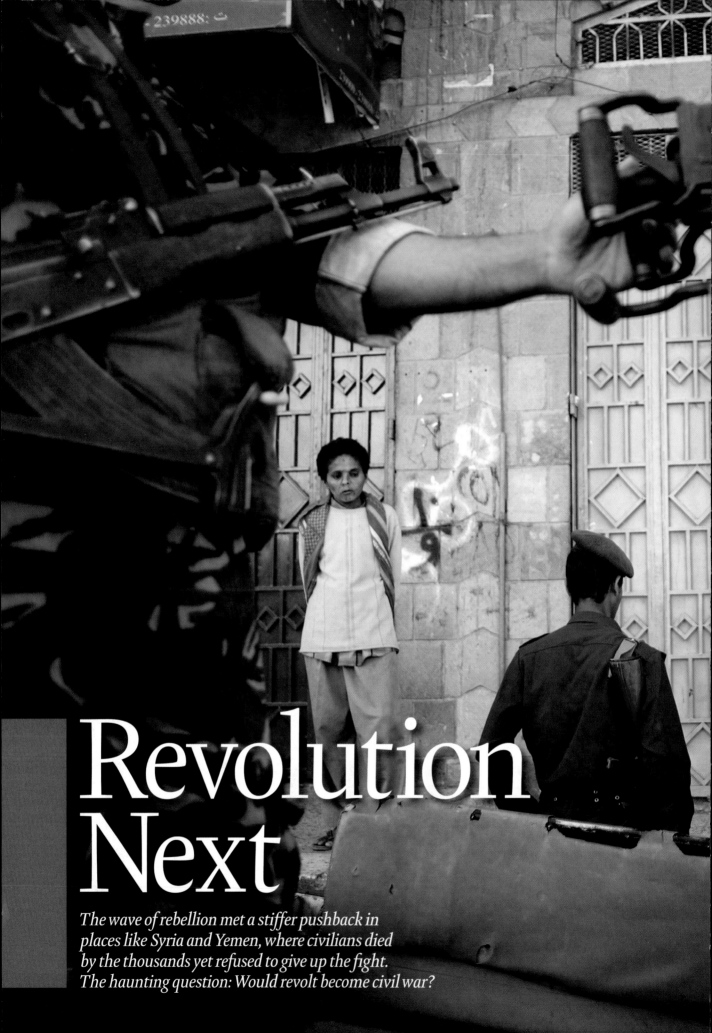

Revolution Next

The wave of rebellion met a stiffer pushback in places like Syria and Yemen, where civilians died by the thousands yet refused to give up the fight. The haunting question: Would revolt become civil war?

Emergency police patrolled the streets of Taiz, Yemen, as unrest in December 2011 turned the streets into a combat zone.

Syria

The Dictator's Brutality

*Determined to buck the trend of the Arab Spring
and hold on to power, Bashar al-Assad put up a
tenacious defense. But the people rising against him
were just as committed to pushing him out.*

BY RANIA ABOUZEID

B
Y THE END OF 2011, THE COST OF STANDING UP TO THE DICTATO-
rial regime of President Bashar al-Assad was abundantly clear to the world.
There was only a trickle of news from Syria—mostly in the form of social media
updates, videos on YouTube, eyewitness accounts of refugees, and the occasional
journalistic foray by reporters—but it was enough to build a composite picture of
the horrors being perpetrated by Assad's troops, intelligence agents, and hired
goons. His tanks were rumbling through cities, soldiers were brutalizing unarmed protesters, even
children were being tortured and murdered.

But Syrians have always known the high price of revolution. The last time anybody challenged the regime was in 1982, when it was headed by Assad's father, Hafez. When the Syrian arm
of the Egyptian-based Islamist group known as the Muslim Brotherhood rose in armed revolt,
the elder Assad responded with maximum brutality. His wrath fell upon the central city of Hama,
where Syrian troops killed at least 10,000 and perhaps as many as 40,000; the exact figure is not
known because the regime was able to impose a near-total blackout of news from Hama. Only ru-
mor and legend remained. According to local lore, Assad ordered one mass grave to be turned into
a car park, such was his contempt for those who dared defy him. Ever since, the massacre served as
a warning against those who would question the absolute authority of the Assads.

That may help explain why Syrians were slow to react to the Arab Spring. In February and
March 2011, calls on Facebook for Tunisian- and Egyptian-style "days of rage" demonstrations
were ignored. For a while, some outside observers thought the winds of change sweeping the Middle East would skirt the country. Yes, Syria shared many of the features that made Tunisia, Egypt,

As demonstrations spread throughout Syria, Bashar al-Assad's regime responded with more and more brutality.

and Libya ripe for revolution: a disproportionately large population under 30, high unemployment, a government riddled by corruption and nepotism, and the absence of basic freedoms. But above all else, Syria was a state governed by an oppressive, almost palpable fear, where the pervasive plainclothes not-so-secret police wanted the people to know that they were being watched. More than a dozen different military and state security intelligence organizations kept close tabs on a cowed populace, as well as on one another.

When some Syrians eventually began to take inspiration from Tunisia and Egypt and demanded greater freedoms, Bashar al-Assad responded just as his father did: with crushing force. But Syria 2011 was not Syria 1982. This time the rebellion was not restricted to one city or one sect. That meant the regime could not concentrate its brutality the way it had been able to do in Hama. Nor could it keep a lid on the news: A blanket ban on foreign journalists did not prevent a constant stream of amateur video from spilling out in social media. Information has consequences: Assad's atrocities compelled the Arab League to suspend Syria's membership, and neighbors like Turkey, formerly a close ally, to shelter those fleeing the violence.

How did Syria get here? When Assad inherited the presidency upon his father's death in 2000, he was just 34, and portrayed himself as a reformer. Unlike his father, whose distant mien mirrored a shrewd ruthlessness, Bashar al-Assad, a British-educated ophthalmologist, cultivated an everyman persona. He dined in Damascene restaurants with his young, glamorous wife. He drove his car himself, and took their three children for strolls through the capital's famed Souq al-Hamidiyah market, and always with a low-security profile.

Assad was closer in age to the country's huge youth population than most of the regime stalwarts from his father's generation. That alone led many to hope he would be able to respond to youthful aspirations and preoccupations. He broke from his father's quasi-socialist worldview and introduced economic policies that encouraged modernization and privatization. Foreign investment arrived from Iran, Turkey, and Lebanon. Assad developed a close relationship with Turkey's prime minister, Recep Tayyip Erdogan, and many Western analysts hoped the Turk would mentor the young autocrat. He also earned popular approval for his strident pro-Palestinian views and hostile foreign policy toward Israel. At the start of 2011, Assad seemed to be sitting pretty. "When there is divergence between your policy and the people's beliefs and interests, you will have this vacuum that creates disturbance," he told the *Wall Street Journal* in January, explaining why he thought his regime was immune to the Arab uprisings. "You have to be very closely linked to the beliefs of the people. This is the core issue."

It was all a chimera. The economic reforms had enriched only a small band of Assad cronies and had failed to provide jobs for the large numbers of young Syrians entering adulthood every year. Assad's Ba'ath Party (related by birth and ideology to Saddam Hussein's Ba'ath Party in Iraq) continued to hold a total monopoly over power, stifling any alternative political aspirations. A decades-old emergency law remained in place, allowing security organizations to intrude into private lives with impunity. All that power was brought to bear at the first sign of dissent.

It began in the impoverished southern city of Dara'a, near the Jordanian border, after some 15 schoolchildren were detained and tortured in March for scribbling anti-regime graffiti. They were writing the mantra of the Arab revolution—"The people want the fall of the regime!"—a slogan that had been repeated from Tunisia to Egypt, from Yemen to Bahrain. The governor of Dara'a came down hard on the kids: Some reports say their fingernails were pulled out.

The severity of the punishment stunned the agricultural community. A tribal elder who petitioned the governor to release the children was told to "forget about these children" and to go and have others. "If you don't know how, send your women, and we'll show you," the governor reportedly said, a quote that quickly spread across the country. "You will regret that," the elder promised.

Protesters took to the city's streets, calling for the governor's dismissal. A crackdown followed, and spread. By the time Assad had fired the governor, ordered the release of the children, and sent a high-ranking delegation to deliver his condolences to the families of those who had died in the rioting, it was too late. The discontent had spread from the south to other parts of the country, stoked by the heavy-handedness of Assad's security forces.

It took Assad two weeks to address his people, and when he did, on March 30, rather than an offer of real reforms, the country was subjected to a display of sycophancy from parliamentarians who interrupted the president's speech with hackneyed pledges of allegiance. Assad's everyman image had begun to unravel: He was exposed as his father's son. Had the dictator offered real reforms in those early days—lifting the emergency law or giving up the Ba'ath Party's monopoly on power—or even simply apologized for protesters' deaths at the hands of his security forces, it is just possible that the uprising could have been contained. He would eventually offer all those things, but by then they were no longer enough for the thousands on the streets. The people wanted the fall of the regime.

As protests grew, the regime responded with more and more violence, as well as wild conspiracy theories to explain the unrest. Blaming the usual bogeymen, Israel and the U.S., rang hollow, so the official Syrian state media suggested that the Arabic satellite channel Al Jazeera had constructed sets in Doha, Qatar, to resemble Syrian cities in order to stage footage of demonstrators being shot at by security forces. To ensure the continued loyalty of the ruling elite, made up mostly of the minority Alawite sect, the regime portrayed the uprisings as the handiwork of extremists within the majority Sunni sect. The country was overrun by rampaging "armed terrorist gangs" and foreigners, state media said.

As the regime ratcheted up the violence, the determination of the protesters seemed to grow. By late summer, when the death toll had climbed into the thousands, protesters were calling for Assad's execution. But it was not yet certain that Assad would go the way of Libya's Muammar Gaddafi, much less Egypt's Hosni Mubarak or Tunisia's Zine El Abidine Ben Ali. He retained a formidable base of support, especially among his fellow Alawites, a group that represents about 12% of Syria's 22 million people.

The country, with its multisectarian, multi-ethnic patchwork society of Christians, Kurds, Alawites, and Sunnis (who make up some 70%), more closely resembles its troubled neighbors Lebanon and Iraq than the relatively homogenous populations of Egypt, Tunisia, or Libya. Still, not all Syrians were equal. Some, especially the Alawites, as well as a select group of elites from other sects, were more equal than others. They were appointed to privileged political and military positions, ensuring a close-knit protective shield around Assad that was based on kinship and shared interests.

The U.S. and the European Union slapped sanctions on Syria and censured some of its key figures in a bid to peel support away from the regime, especially from its upper echelons and from the merchant classes of the country's two largest cities, the capital, Damascus, and Aleppo, which had largely stayed on the sidelines during the turmoil. Still, the uncertainty of what might come after Assad kept many Syrians on his side. Bashar al-Assad, like Hafez, has long touted himself as the guarantor of the rights of Syria's many minorities. The Assads may have wielded iron fists, but they had also given the country four decades of domestic stability, something many Syrians were loath to risk. They didn't have to look far to see how ugly wholesale regime change could be. Their country hosts over a million refugees from the post-Saddam violence in Iraq. Lebanon offers another cautionary tale with its various quarreling sects and perennially unstable politics. For

In Jabal al-Zawiya, popular resistance is organizing demonstrations and the funerals of its martyrs. The events are protected by the Free Syrian Army, which is securing this part of the country.

some Syrians the oft-trotted-out mantra of Arab strongmen—it's me and stability, or freedom and chaos—seemed a pretty good deal given their tumultuous neighborhood.

But many Syrians no longer wanted that deal: The ranks of the protesters were swelling. Assad's crackdown did not have the effect he desired, and the ubiquity of his spies and security officers may actually have strengthened the resolve of demonstrators: They knew their participation had been noted and documented, and terrible punishment awaited them if they failed.

To succeed in revolution or its aftermath, the protesters will need a good deal more unity. The Syrian opposition, a disparate group of aging intellectuals, exiled Islamists, and Kurds, have struggled to form a single anti-Assad front. There is a disconnect between opposition leaders outside and inside the country.

Pro-government demonstrators rally in Damascus to denounce the Arab League's suspension of Syria's membership.

But by the end of 2011 another type of opposition was forming. Defectors from Assad's army, mainly low-ranking Sunni conscripts, had banded into the so-called Free Syrian Army and begun to take the fight back to the regime, fueling fears of civil war.

Syria's location means its unraveling could have wide and unpredictable consequences. A sectarian war, one possible outcome, could drag in its tinderbox neighbors, Lebanon and Iraq. An isolated Assad may feel compelled to lash out at Israel to divert the people's attention. Iran, which would hate to lose its most steadfast ally in the Arab world, might play the role of spoiler. Russia and China resisted stronger international action against Damascus, even as the U.S. moved to shut down its embassy there. But with so many of Assad's people showing a determination to pay revolution's ultimate price, a return to old certainties may be out of the question.

Yemen

More Wars to Wage

Getting rid of the dictator was just the first step.
The poorest nation on the Arabian peninsula
is racked by internal conflicts that
could spill out into the wider world.

BY BOBBY GHOSH

VERY TYRANT TAKEN DOWN BY 2011'S ARAB
Spring departed differently: Tunisia's Zine El Abidine Ben
Ali fled into exile, Egypt's Hosni Mubarak wound up in
court, Libya's Muammar Gaddafi met the ugliest end. But
Yemen's Ali Abdullah Saleh, having endured nearly a year of
protests and survived a rocket attack on his palace, got the
closest thing to an honorable discharge for dictators. In November 2011 he
signed a deal brokered by the Gulf Cooperation Council that would let him
leave office after nearly 34 years in power and be immune from prosecution.

Saleh's contentious exit promises more instability in what is already
one of the most dangerous countries in the world. Impoverished Yemen has
for years been racked by three low-intensity wars, each of which threatens
to explode into a major conflict at a moment's notice. In the South, where
many feel they don't get a fair share of the country's resources, there's a
militant movement dedicated to returning to the pre-1990 arrangement
of two separate Yemens. (Unifying the conservative North with the social-
ist South was Saleh's biggest achievement.) In the far north on the border with Saudi Arabia is a seven-year-old insurgency by Houthis, a radical
Shi'ite sect whose adherents want to impose Islamist rule.

And then there's al Qaeda in the Arabian Peninsula, or AQAP, the
global terrorist group's most ambitious franchise: It was behind virtually

Change Square in the capital of Sanaa became the locus of antigovernment protests for thousands of Yemenites.

every major terrorist plot uncovered in the U.S. and Europe during the past three years, including 2010's plot to use the global airfreight network to deliver bombs to Chicago and an attempt to blow up a passenger jet over Detroit on Christmas Day 2009. AQAP also tried to assassinate a prominent Saudi prince. The U.S. drone attack in September 2011 that killed the radical AQAP cleric Anwar al-Awlaki did not deter his fellow jihadists. With Saleh's attention distracted by the uprising against him and the military split on whether to support the president, AQAP greatly expanded its reach within Yemen. Its ambitions may have grown too. Some officials fear the group will now seek to impose a Taliban-style rule on the country.

All this bodes ill for a country ranked 172nd in the world in per capita GDP, and one running low on oil reserves and with a fast-growing population (more than 70% of its 24 million people are younger than 30) facing dismal economic prospects.

In recent years Saleh's economic planners woke to the challenges posed by the youth bulge and sought to goose the economy into creating jobs. They tried, for instance, to capitalize on the

Fallen icon: Images of longtime dictator Saleh adorn a shop in the old town of Sanaa.

cooler temperatures of the capital, Sanaa, to market it as a place for Arabs from other countries to build summer homes. But investment has been fitful, and unemployment remains astronomical: Nearly half of Yemenis ages 15 to 29 are neither going to school nor employed.

Those problems are compounded by massive institutional graft. According to Transparency International, Yemen is one of the most corrupt countries on the planet. It requires no great stretch of the imagination to see Yemen becoming like Afghanistan in the violent years after the end of Soviet occupation. Can that dire fate be avoided? The young men and women who rose against Saleh in 2011 represent the country's best hope of building anew. Although not as blessed as resource-rich Saudi Arabia and Oman, Yemen does have great potential in seafood and tourism. Those wealthy neighbors have an interest in developing the Yemeni economy, not least because they fear massive inflows of immigrants. Western nations, acutely aware of the AQAP threat, are keen to help. There's hope, too, that a democratic Yemen will attract investment from a large diaspora in Europe, the U.S., and other Gulf countries.

None of that is possible without political stability. Any post-Saleh government must swiftly persuade southern separatists to remain in the union and must disarm the Houthis. A deal is required to unify the pro- and anti-Saleh elements of the military. And the fight against AQAP will probably be long and hard. With so many crises at hand, it's hard to know where the new Yemeni government will begin. Saleh's exit deal left many questions unanswered as this book went to press. Crucially, it was unclear whether Saleh's family would go with him; his son and nephews control powerful security organizations and extensive business empires. And what will happen to the many loyalists he placed in important government positions or rewarded with business interests? Who will be held accountable for the hundreds of protesters killed during the anti-Saleh uprising?

For its neighbors and the West, the priority is dealing with the terrorist threat. U.S. counterterrorism experts reckon that AQAP's capabilities, measured by the sophistication of its tactics and its ability to execute operations outside its own territory, are roughly equivalent to those of bin Laden's original group in the late 1990s. That was the period when al Qaeda announced itself to the world by bombing the U.S. embassies in Nairobi and Dar es Salaam. There's plenty of evidence that AQAP's goals are growing progressively grander. Taking advantage of the uprising against Saleh, the group has been able to raid and loot military ammunition depots, adding to its already considerable arsenal. It even briefly took control of a major southern town.

Saleh's departure is also likely to embolden both the southern separatists and the Houthis in the North. That, in turn, could create alarm across the Arabian peninsula: Sunni-majority Saudi Arabia, already anxious about the Shi'ite uprising in Bahrain, regards the Houthis as dangerous heretics. Northern Yemenis say that Saudi forces have on occasion crossed the border to strike at Houthis. Needless to say, all those problems will be exacerbated by Yemen's worsening economy. Of the countries liberated by the Arab Spring, Yemen faces the hardest path to stable democracy. Saleh once said that running his country was akin to "dancing on the head of snakes." His successor had better have nimble feet.

What America Can Do

BY JOE KLEIN

O NE OF THE MORE REMARKABLE ASPECTS OF THE ARAB SPRING, FROM an American point of view, is that Barack Obama saw it coming. More than six months before Tahrir Square became iconic, the President gathered several of his Middle East specialists and asked them to consider what U.S. policy should be if autocratic dynasties like Mubarak's in Egypt and the Assads' in Syria began to teeter. The team's report, not quite completed when Mohamed Bouazizi set himself ablaze in Tunisia, pointed to quiet support of American values—freedom, democracy—in the region, without an aggressive military intervention.

And that is what Obama has done. It has not always been successful—Syria remains a bloody muddle, and there are more questions than answers in Egypt, Libya, and Yemen—but Obama's patience has enabled the U.S. to engage the region in a more thoughtful, nuanced way than the brutish insensitivity that has characterized Western attitudes toward Arab lands since the end of World War I.

Now comes the hard part. The early, breathtaking exhilaration of seeing Arabs risk their lives for freedom is over. Mubarak and Gaddafi are gone, but the economic paralysis, crude educational systems, and embedded oligarchies remain. These countries are not fertile soil for democracy, at least not yet. They lack a strong middle class, and they have to build supple traditions of free speech and justice. Some of them may not even be countries.

The straight-line borders drawn by the European powers after World War I paid no heed to the actual tribal boundaries that divided these lands. Countries like Libya, Iraq, Jordan, Syria, and Israel were slapdash figments of the Western imagination—and all of the above, except Israel, may find that, absent an autocrat, there isn't that much to bind them together. The United States faces impossible choices: which tribes, or coalitions of tribes, or religious sects to support. The Libyan intervention was an impossible decision, made easier by the presence of the archvillain Gaddafi. If Syria now descends into a Sunni-Alawite civil war, if Iraq's majority Shi'ites begin a massacre of Sunnis in al-Anbar province, if Jordan's Palestinians and Hashem-

Obama at the Great Pyramid of Giza in June 2009, when he addressed the Muslim world from Cairo

ites decide to square off, the choice for the United States and its allies will be far more difficult.

Chaos is a strong possibility for the region, but not the only one. A simpleminded American looks at Egypt's parliamentary election results, sees 70% of the seats going to Islamists, and assumes trouble. It is true that the Muslim Brotherhood and Salafists may form a hegemonic, anti-Western majority. But it's possible that the antidemocratic extremism of the Salafis will isolate them from a democratic majority composed of the Islamists and the secularists who joined together in Tahrir Square. It is also possible that the Egyptian military will fear the uncertainty and roil that comes with democracy and decide to maintain the status quo—army rule—that has obtained since 1952.

How should the United States react to all this? With humility and patience, with diplomacy and humanitarian support. Unfortunately, after a decade of unseemly intervention in Iraq and quagmire in Afghanistan, we no longer have either the economic wherewithal or diplomatic credibility to be a defining force in the region. Yes, there will be a military response if essential U.S. interests—the flow of oil, the existence of Israel—are threatened. But we lack the economic power to launch a Middle Eastern version of the Marshall Plan, which is the single most important thing we could do to stabilize the region. Indeed, with our European allies in danger of economic collapse, our best option is to try to persuade the oil-rich Gulf kingdoms to act in their own long-term best interest and finance a huge jobs and infrastructure program. So far, they have not shown much inclination to do so.

It is an awkward and unusual position for an American government. But that doesn't mean we are powerless. We do have the power of example. Obama's decision to back the Libyan rebels was wildly popular in the region. And we have the power of our ideals: The ideal of the Tahrir Square masses, the dream of the Tunisian fruit seller, the goal of the brave Syrians facing Assad's army in the streets, was to have the same freedoms that we have. The United States has not always acted according to its values in the Middle East, but now—after so many mistakes—our principles are the last bastion of strength, the best hope for influence, that we still possess.

About
the Authors

RANIA ABOUZEID is a print, television, radio, and multimedia journalist based in Beirut. She has a dozen years of experience in the Middle East and Pakistan, covering the region for TIME and other publications.

REZA ASLAN is the founder of AslanMedia.com, an online portal for news and information about the Middle East. His books include *No god but God, Beyond Fundamentalism*, and *Tablet & Pen*.

ARYN BAKER is TIME's Middle East bureau chief and has covered the region since 2011. She also writes about Pakistan and Afghanistan, which she has covered since 2003. She is based in Beirut, where she focuses on Islam, culture, politics, and conflict throughout the greater Middle East.

CLEO BROCK-ABRAHAM is a TIME magazine reporter who has worked extensively on the magazine's coverage of the Arab Spring. After teaching English in Cairo in 2007, she pursued a master's in Middle Eastern studies from the School of Oriental and African Studies in London.

APARISIM "BOBBY" GHOSH is TIME's deputy international editor and a writer on global affairs. He has spent more than a decade covering the greater Middle East, writing cover stories on conflict, religion, and revolution.

ABIGAIL HAUSLOHNER is TIME's correspondent in Egypt, and has covered the Middle East—from Iraq to Libya, Tunisia, Yemen, and the Gaza Strip—for TIME since 2008.

JOE KLEIN is TIME's political columnist and an editor-at-large. He has been traveling to the Middle East for more than 30 years, covering wars and elections in Israel, Iran, Iraq, Lebanon, Syria, and Egypt.

YURI KOZYREV is an award-winning photojournalist who has covered the Middle East for TIME since 2001. In that time, he has photographed the wars in Afghanistan and Iraq, the civil war in Libya, and the Arab Spring uprisings across the region. He is based in Moscow.

ISHAAN THAROOR is a writer for TIME magazine and Time.com and editor of Global Spin, TIME's international affairs blog.

KARL VICK is TIME's Jerusalem bureau chief, covering Israel and the Palestinian territories. He has previously reported from Iraq, Iran, Afghanistan, Yemen, Jordan, Turkey, Pakistan, Kosovo, Kyrgyzstan, and much of Africa.

VIVIENNE WALT is a TIME contributor who reported on the revolutions in Tunisia, Egypt, and Libya. She covered the Iraq War, and has written from Yemen, Syria, Palestine, Morocco, Sudan, and much of Africa.